"MULTIPLICATION IS FOR WHITE PEOPLE"

Also by Lisa Delpit
Other People's Children

Edited by Lisa Delpit
The Real Ebonics Debate (with Theresa Perry)
The Skin That We Speak (with Joanne Kilgour Dowdy)

"MULTIPLICATION IS FOR WHITE PEOPLE"

RAISING EXPECTATIONS FOR OTHER PEOPLE'S CHILDREN

Lisa Delpit

The publisher has made every effort to contact all rights holders of reprinted material in *"Multiplication Is for White People"*. If notified, the publisher will be pleased to rectify any omission in future editions.

First published in the United States by The New Press, New York, 2012
This paperback edition published by The New Press, 2013
Distributed by Perseus Distribution

ISBN 978-1-59558-898-2 (pbk.)
ISBN 978-1-59558-770-1 (e-book)

LIBRARY OF CONGRESS CATALOGING-IN-PUBLICATION DATA

Delpit, Lisa D.
  "Multiplication is for white people": raising expectations for other people's children / Lisa Delpit.
    p. cm.
  Includes bibliographical references.
  ISBN 978-1-59558-046-7 (hc.)
  1. Educational equalization--United States. 2. Academic achievement--United States.
3. African American students. 4. Minorities--Education--United States. 5. Students with social disabilities--Education--United States. 6. United States--Race relations. I. Title.
  LC213.2.D45 2011
  379.2'60973--dc23
                                        2011042727

The New Press publishes books that promote and enrich public discussion and understanding of the issues vital to our democracy and to a more equitable world. These books are made possible by the enthusiasm of our readers; the support of a committed group of donors, large and small; the collaboration of our many partners in the independent media and the not-for-profit sector; booksellers, who often hand-sell New Press books; librarians; and above all by our authors.

www.thenewpress.com

Composition by The Influx House

Printed in the United States of America

10 9 8 7 6 5 4

This book is dedicated to my mother, Edmae Butler, a ninety-six-year-old educator who is still teaching me patience, unconditional love, and the value of finding something to laugh at every day;

To my daughter, Maya Delpit, who—as she constantly reminds me— taught me everything I know about teaching "other people's children";

To my Southern University students who continue their commitment to education in the face of challenges that would leave lesser people hiding under their covers;

And to the brilliant and talented students of Southern University Laboratory School, their teachers, principal, and families.

CONTENTS

ACKNOWLEDGMENTS

This book has been a long time coming and would not have seen the printer's press were it not for Diane Wachtell, my editor, publisher, and friend. In addition to her unflagging encouragement during my most frustrating times, she also refused—on multiple occasions—to take back the book advance! Many thanks as well to Tara Grove and Cinqué Hicks, who nurtured the process to completion.

That I was able to keep working on a manuscript during difficult work and personal times is due in large part to the young and not-so-young teachers who consistently nourished my soul with their commitment to social justice and to African American children. Patricia Lesesne, Makeesha Coleman, Anrea Williams, Tiffany Pogue, Shayne Evans, and so many other young African American educators I have been honored to encounter, your tireless efforts to give our children brighter futures is exhausting to watch, but so inspires me to continue the struggle. Hannah Sadtler, Derek Roguski, and Dave Stieber, you, along with many others I have had the privilege to meet, prove the ability to transcend racial identities, eschew racial privilege, and work for the good of all humanity.

I would like to thank Rodrick Jenkins for sharing with me his voluminous research findings on the effects of desegregation on black educators. Rodrick, you will make an excellent professor!

I must also thank my family for their support, especially my goddaughter and niece Loren Brown, my sister-in-law Precious Delpit, and my nephew Joseph Delpit Jr., who selflessly devoted time to help me during a very difficult transition. My cousin Wanda Shakesnider allows everyone in the family to focus on what needs to be done because she keeps my mother smiling, under the loving eye of my sister, Billie Cunningham.

I would also like to thank all of my friends who have helped me during the often tedious writing process. Joan Wynne sent innumerable emails to keep me on track. Harry Amana provided a dedicated writing getaway space and kept me entertained when I needed a break. To all of my wonderful, talented, supportive friends, you are a constant and appreciated blessing.

Finally, I would like to express great appreciation to Ragdale, which provided a residency that allowed me to focus solely on writing in the company of a group of creative and exciting colleagues.

INTRODUCTION:
YES, DIANE, I'M STILL ANGRY

Recently I was invited by education activist Dr. Raynard Sanders to New Orleans for an educational summit. The speaker, the renowned and controversial Diane Ravitch, had told Dr. Sanders that she wanted to meet me. Dr. Ravitch, currently a professor at New York University, has made headlines with her about-face on many issues related to public education. Ravitch was the assistant secretary of education in the George H.W. Bush administration, where she made her conservative intellectual and political reputation with her staunch support of standardized testing, charter schools, the No Child Left Behind Act, and free market competition for schools. She has now repudiated many of her earlier positions, stated both in public presentations and in her book *The Death and Life of the Great American School System: How Testing and Choice Are Undermining Education*. This courageous scholar has resigned from influential conservative policy groups and has incited many powerful enemies. As a result, in contrast to her former life as a popular conservative commentator, she has now found herself barred from expressing her new views in many popular venues.

Before the speech began, I joined Diane, Raynard, and a few invited guests in an adjoining room. Diane and I talked about the devastation of public schools in post-Katrina New Orleans and how politicians and educational entrepreneurs hawking privatization are claiming the travesty of New Orleans education to be a national model.

Diane asked me why I hadn't spoken out nationally against what was happening. I told her about my work in New Orleans and my modestly successful attempts to engage other African American scholars in the struggle against what was happening there. I added that the sense of futility in the battle for rational education policy for African American children had gone on for so long and that I had come to feel so tired, that I now needed to focus on those areas where I felt I could actually make a difference: working with teachers and children in an African American school. I was so angry from the sensation of butting my head against a brick wall, I told her, that I needed to give my "anger muscles" a rest. Diane looked at me squarely and said, "You don't *look* angry."

I realized two things at that moment. One was that Diane's anger was relatively raw and still fresh and hadn't yet needed to be modulated. It must have been quite a shock to go from being an influential authority whose views were sought and valued in most political circles to being a virtual outcast. While it was undeniably courageous to reanalyze one's positions and come to a significantly different stance, it has to be anger-provoking to realize that the power elite seem less interested in logical analyses for the public good than in maintaining power and profit. Her anger had a different quality than the anger of those of us who have struggled with the same issues for many years.

The second thing I realized was that, yes, I *am* still angry—despite my attempts over the years to calm my spirit and to focus on the wonder of teaching and learning. I am angry at the machinations of those who, with so little knowledge of learning, of teachers, or of children, are twisting the life out of schools.

I am angry that public schools, once a beacon of democracy, have been overrun by the antidemocratic forces of extreme wealth. Educational policy for the past decade has largely been determined by the financial contributions of several very large corporate foundations. Among a few others, the Broad, Gates, and Walton (Walmart) foundations have dictated various "reforms" by flooding the educational enterprise with capital. The ideas of privatization, charter schools, Teach for America, the extremes of the accountability movement, merit pay, increased standardized testing, free market competition—all are promulgated and financially supported by corporate foundations, which indeed *have* those funds because they can avoid paying the taxes that the rest of us must foot. Thus, educational policy has been virtually hijacked by the wealthiest citizens, whom no one elected and who are unlikely ever to have had a child in the public schools.

I am angry that with all of the corporate and taxpayers' money that is flowing into education, little-to-none is going to those valiant souls who have toiled in urban educational settings for many years with proven track records. Instead, money typically goes to those with little exposure to and even less experience in urban schools. I am left in my more cynical moments with the thought that poor black children have become the vehicle by which rich white people give money to their friends.

I am angry because of the way that the original idea of charter schools has been corrupted. In their first iteration, charter schools were to be beacons for what could happen in public schools. They were intended to develop models for working with the most challenging populations. What they discovered was to be shared and reproduced in other public school classrooms. Now, because of the insertion of the "market model," charter schools often shun the very students they were intended to help. Special education students, students with behavioral issues, and students who need any kind of special assistance are excluded in a multiplicity of ways because they reduce the bottom line—they lower test scores and take more time to educate properly. Charter schools have any number of ways of "counseling" such students out of their programs. I have been told by parents that many charter schools accuse students of a series of often trivial rule infractions, then tell parents that the students will not be suspended if the parents voluntarily transfer them to another school. Parents of a student with special needs are told that the charter is not prepared to meet their child's needs adequately and that he or she would be much better served at the regular public school around the corner. (Schools in New Orleans, the "model city" for charters, have devised an even more sinister scheme for keeping unwanted children out of the schools. The K–12 publicly funded charter schools, which are supposed to be open to all through a lottery system of enrollment, are giving preferential admission to children who have attended an affiliated private preschool, one of which charges over $4,000 in tuition and the other over $9,000.)[1]

In addition, the market-driven model insists that should charter schools actually discover workable, innovative ideas, they are not to be shared with other public schools but held close to the vest to prevent "competitors" from "winning" the standardized test race. So now, charter schools are not meant to contribute to "regular" public education but to put it out of business.

I am angry about the hypocrisy rampant in education policy. While schools and teachers are admonished to adhere to research-based instruction and data-driven planning, there is no research to support the proliferation of charter schools, pay-for-performance plans, or market-based school competition. Indeed, where there is research, it largely suggests that we should do an about-face and run in the opposite direction.

I am angry that the conversation about educating our children has become so restricted. What has happened to the societal desire to instill character? To develop creativity? To cultivate courage and kindness? How can we look at a small bundle of profound potential and see only a number describing inadequacy? Why do we punish our children with our inability to teach them? How can we live with the fact that in Miami—and I am certain in many other cities—ten-year-olds facing failure on the state-mandated FCAT test and being "left back" in third grade for the third time, have had to be restrained from committing suicide?

I am angry at what the inflexibility and wrong-headed single-mindedness of schools in this era have done to my child and to so many other children. There is little tolerance for difference, for creativity, or for challenge.

The current use of standardized tests, which has the goals of promoting competition between schools and of making teacher and principal salaries—and sometimes even employment—dependent on tests scores, seems to bring out the worst in adults as well. In locale after locale—including Washington, DC; Georgia; Indiana; Massachusetts; Nevada; and Virginia, to name a few—there are investigations into widespread allegations of cheating by teachers and principals on state-mandated high-stakes tests.

And finally—if there ever *is* a finally—I am angry at the racism that, despite having a president who is half white and half black, still permeates our America. In my earlier days, I wrote about the problem of cultural conflict—that one of the reasons that having teachers and children of different cultural groups led to difficulties in teaching and learning was a lack of understanding about the other group's culture. I now have a slightly different perspective. I still believe that the problem is cultural, but it is larger than the children or their teachers. The problem is that the cultural framework of our country has, almost since its inception, dictated that "black" is bad and less than and in all arenas "white" is good and superior. This perspective is so ingrained and so normalized that we all stumble through our days with eyes closed to avoid seeing it. We miss the pain in our children's eyes when they have internalized the societal belief that they are dumb, unmotivated, and dispensable.

Nor can we see what happens to the psyches of young, often well-meaning white people who have been told that they are the best and brightest and that they are the saviors of black children. Most inevitably fail because they haven't the training or the experience to navigate such unfamiliar territory successfully; nor are they taught to learn with humility from parents or from veteran African American and other teachers who know the children and the communities in which they teach. Others burn out quickly from carrying the weight of salvation that has been piled upon their young shoulders. Several young Teach for America recruits have told me that their colleagues frequently run back home or off to graduate school with the belief that the children they went to save are unsalvageable—not because of poor teaching but because of their students' parents, families, or communities.

Yes, Diane, I am still angry. And that anger has fueled the two themes that run throughout this book. The first is the symbiotic interplay between my personal life as a mother and my professional work as a scholar and hopeful activist. Within the chapters of this volume are stories that range from my daughter Maya's first years in elementary school through her admission to college. My concerns for her educational struggles informed my work in schools. Feeling her frustration and pain opened my eyes to the frustration and pain thriving in so many of the classrooms I visited. Reveling in her successes helped me to suggest potential modifications for schools where I saw damaging practices. In fact, Maya has more than once over the years informed me that I wouldn't know half as much about education if I didn't have her! And she's right.

The second theme that runs through the book, from the chapters on educating young children to those focused on college students, is the relevance of a list of ten factors I have formulated over a number of years that I believe can foster excellence in urban classrooms. These factors encapsulate my beliefs about black children and learning, about creating classrooms that speak to children's strengths rather than hammering them with their weaknesses, and about building connections to cultures and communities. I believe that if we are to create excellence in urban classrooms, we must do the following:

1. Recognize the importance of a teacher and good teaching, especially for the "school dependent" children of low-income communities.
2. Recognize the brilliance of poor, urban children and teach them *more* content, not less.
3. Whatever methodology or instructional program is used, demand critical thinking while at the same time assuring that all children gain access to "basic skills"— the conventions and strategies that are essential to success in American society.
4. Provide children with the emotional ego strength to challenge racist societal views of their own competence and worthiness and that of their families and communities.
5. Recognize and build on children's strengths.
6. Use familiar metaphors and experiences from the children's world to connect what students already know to school-taught knowledge.
7. Create a sense of family and caring in the classroom.
8. Monitor and assess students' needs and then address them with a wealth of diverse strategies.
9. Honor and respect the children's home cultures.

10. Foster a sense of children's connection to community, to something greater than themselves.

So, yes, Diane, I am still angry. But I am also still hopeful. Some days I find it easier than others to locate that hope, so I am thankful that I have the opportunity to spend most of my days with the African American children at Southern University Laboratory School. There is nothing to inspire hope like the beaming smile of a kindergartner who has just written her first book or the cool demeanor that can't quite mask the excited grin of a seventh grader who has just mastered quadratic equations or a senior trembling with exhilaration and anticipation as he flashes his first college acceptance letter. No matter how angry I get when I think about what the larger world may have in store for them, I owe my life to children, and I am forever grateful for the hope and joy their smiles and hugs engender.

"MULTIPLICATION IS FOR WHITE PEOPLE"

PART ONE
INHERENT ABILITY

1

THERE IS NO ACHIEVEMENT GAP AT BIRTH

Many reasons have been given for why African American children are not excelling in schools in the United States. One that is seldom spoken aloud, but that is buried within the American psyche, is that black children are innately less capable—that they are somehow inferior. I want to start by dispelling that myth.

In 1956, French researcher Marcelle Geber, under a research grant from the United Nations Children's Fund, traveled to Africa in order to study the effects of malnutrition on infant and child development. Geber concentrated on Kenya and Uganda, where she made a momentous discovery: despite the expectation that malnutrition would cause lower rates of infant development, the developmental rate of native Ugandan infants was so much higher than the established norm that these babies were able to outperform European children twice or three times their age.

Geber found, in her words, the most precocious and advanced infants ever observed anywhere in the world. She saw four-day-old infants who smiled continuously. She published photographs of a forty-eight-hour-old child bolt upright, supported only by his forearms, head in perfect balance, and eyes focused. At six to seven weeks, all the children crawled skillfully and sat up by themselves.

The Ugandan infants were months ahead of children of European descent on any intelligence scale utilized. Based on the Gesell tests for early intelligence developed at Yale University, Geber showed infants between six and seven months old a toy, then walked across the room and put the toy into a tall toy box. The African children would leap up, walk quietly across the room, reach into the basket, and retrieve the toy. Beyond the extraordinary sensory-motor skills of walking and retrieval, the test shows that "object permanency" had occurred in the child's developing mind—the first great shift of logical processing.[1]

In the mid-1960s in the United States, William Frankenburg, a professor of pediatrics and preventive medicine, and fellow researcher Joe Dodds were intrigued to find that black American children as young as six months old developed significantly more quickly than did white American infants. Frankenburg and Dodds found the results interesting but perhaps merely some sort of data quirk and not replicable. The researchers, who worked together for more than twenty years, decided to crunch the numbers on thousands of children years later. Once again they were astounded. "There were no items that the white children were doing earlier than the black children in the first year of life," Dodds notes. Even by age four, blacks had an edge in fifteen categories, while whites bested blacks in only three. Dodds continued, "These were two studies removed by years and totally different samples of kids. To come up with some of the same trends, I didn't believe we would find that."[2] One researcher has even suggested that the faster maturation of black babies continues during the early months even when the children suffer from poverty and poor diet.[3]

More recently, in her 2006 University of Iowa dissertation, Phyllis Rippeyoung looked at scores of African American and white infants on the Bayley Scale of Infant Development. When she looked at the race of the mother and incorporated a number of socioeconomic and demographic controls, she found that black infants got slightly higher cognitive-skill scores and considerably higher motor-skill scores. In other words, she found that if black and white babies were born with the same degree of good health, and the parents interacted with the babies to the same degree, black babies would surpass white babies on all aspects of the Bayley Scale.

I do not raise these studies to somehow suggest the superiority of black children. Differences between the two groups tend to even out prior to schooling. The data thus far collected indicate that African American and European American children tend to equalize abilities by about age four or five, after which many of the trends tend to reverse. Some suggest that the environmental conditions of poverty and/or racism then create conditions that the initial advantage of black children cannot overcome.[4] It is also conceivable that inappropriate schooling has the effect of reducing continued progress.

I write these words because what we need to know at a very deep level is that African American children do not come into this world at a deficit. There is no "achievement gap" at birth— at least not one that favors European American children. Indeed, the achievement gap should not be considered the gap between black children's performance and white children's performance— the latter of which can be considered only mediocre on an international scale—but rather between black children's performance and these same children's exponentially greater potential. When we educators look out at a classroom of black faces, we must understand that we are looking at children at least as brilliant as those from any well-to-do white community. If we do not recognize the brilliance before us, we cannot help but carry on the stereotypic societal views that these children are somehow damaged goods and that they cannot be expected to succeed.

What happens when we assume that certain children are less than brilliant? Our tendency is to teach less, to teach down, to teach for remediation. Without having any intention of discriminating, we can do harm to children who are viewed within a stereotype of "less than"—"Those poor little children suffering in those low-income homes, with no fathers, with the violence in the communities, with no one to help them with their homework; we can't expect too much of them. If we have to test them, it's in their best interest to encourage them to stay home on testing days so they won't be stressed."

I think often of a principal who shared a story with me about one of her charges in an inner-city elementary school. Five-year-old African American Nelson always seemed to end up being sent to the principal's office. The principal found him to be a delightful, intelligent little boy and found it hard to understand why he was always getting into so much trouble. One day she sat him down to have a heart-to-heart. "Nelson, what happened today?" "Ms. B., I'm just sick of them li'l p's. She always giving me them li'l p's. And then, when I finish one page, here she come with more. I'm just tired of it, Ms. B.; I'm just sick of them li'l p's!" Rather than supply Nelson with challenging, exciting material, the teacher believed he needed rote repetition of skills he had clearly already mastered. If we are serious about having all children succeed, we cannot allow them to wallow in metaphorical l'il p's because they have been determined to be a part of the group that can only learn l'il p's. Rather, we must acknowledge the quality of the raw materials we're working with and teach to these children's inherent genius.

Another excuse for poor performance has been the rationale that African Americans are part of a "culture of poverty." This is a model of deficit thinking, popularized by the work of Ruby Payne: something is wrong with the children who are in the classroom, if not in their genes, then in their culture.[5] The Payne "culture of poverty" model as the cause of poor school performance by low-income children and children of color has now been adopted by school districts around the country. Indeed, in order to meet the demand, Payne in 2006 employed twenty-five trainers and provided additional work for fifty consultants nationwide. It is convenient to choose poverty as the reason for poor performance—attaching poor academic performance to factors such as the number of parents in the household, the educational background of the mother, or the level of poverty in the community. These are things we in the schools cannot change, and, as Jawanza Kunjufu suggests in *An African Centered Response to Ruby Payne's Poverty Theory*, blaming poverty works out for school systems because then you don't have to change your lesson plans![6]

This kind of thinking harkens back to the old cultural-deficit arguments of the 1960s and 1970s. William Ryan, in his 1971 book *Blaming the Victim*, forcefully critiqued this notion:

> In education we have compensatory education to build up the skills and attitudes of the ghetto child rather than structural changes in the schools. In race relations we have social engineers to think up ways to strengthen the Negro family rather than methods of eradicating racism.[7]

I don't disagree with all of Payne's suggestions, such as creating relationships between teachers and students, which, of course, is critical. Many of the suggestions are good ones that teachers and schools should adopt. But I disagree with her overall analysis and therefore find the solutions she offers very limited. What Payne is labeling *culture* is actually the response to oppression. True culture supports its people; it doesn't destroy them.

This reminds me of a white graduate student who came to me very upset as she tried to figure something out. She lived in a native village in Alaska, a place where there is often a problem with alcohol abuse. She told me of a man who would get drunk all the time and beat his wife and his dogs. The graduate student was just horrified. She went to talk to her professor, who was one of the people who was supposed to teach her how to work within different cultures, and this person said to her, "Well, you shouldn't get upset about that because that's their culture." When the student told me the professor's response, I was very angry, and I told her so. It is critical that we figure out the difference between culture and a response to oppression. Beating your wife is no one's culture. It is a response to a situation—in this case possibly the racism prevalent in Alaska against Native Alaskans and the minimal opportunities for Native Alaskan men to either maintain their traditional subsistence lifestyles or to find a place within the more recent cash economy. It is no more acceptable to condone such behavior than to blame poor academic performance on a "culture of poverty."

So, if genetics and culture are not the problem, what is?

There are several related issues that I would like to discuss. The first is a very simple one, an elegant example of the scientific "law of parsimony," which states that in looking to find the most likely cause for research findings, it is often best to accept the simplest explanation rather than more complicated alternatives. One reason for the lack of African American academic success in schools is that many poor African American students are simply not being taught.

After many visits to many American schools, I can say with confidence that in the schools where children are performing at high levels, a large number of teachers are actually teaching. They are very visible in the classroom. They have the children's attention. They are explaining concepts and using metaphors that connect the knowledge children bring to school with the new information the children are learning; for example, the teacher in Louisiana who compared how neurons work in the human body with how cell phone systems work. These teachers use different kinds of media. They ask students to explain concepts to their peers. They ask questions that require deep thought, and they demand responses.

In many schools where children are not performing, a larger number of teachers are not really teaching (although there are almost always exceptional teachers to be found in any school setting). The children are completing worksheets, answering written questions, doing seat work. The teachers are at their own desks, apparently also doing seat work. There is little interaction except for discipline. Few questions are asked, and those that are asked demand little thought. Children who choose not to be involved are ignored.

I cannot stress enough how important teaching is. Good teaching is desirable, but *any* teaching is preferable to classrooms where teachers have abdicated the role completely. And *good* teaching is miraculous. William Sanders and J.C. Rivers, in their 1996 study on the effects of good teachers, compared students who had three good teachers in a row with students who had three weaker teachers in a row as each group took third-, fourth-, and fifth-grade math. The students who had good teachers performed fifty percentile points above those with weaker teachers! Bearing in mind that the so-called achievement gap is usually about fifteen points, what would scoring fifty percentile points higher mean about such a gap? Such is the power of good teaching![8]

A second reason African American students are not excelling is that we have all been affected by our society's deeply ingrained bias of equating blackness with inferiority. It would not take much research to identify individuals, praised by the larger society, who have embraced this point of view. Here are but a few examples from noted citizens:

A Black, after a hard labour through the day, will be induced by the slightest amusements to sit up till midnight, or later, though knowing he must be out with the first dawn of the morning.

... They are more ardent after their female: but love seems with them to be more an eager desire, than a tender, delicate mixture of sentiment and sensation.

... Their griefs are transient. . . . Afflictions . . . are less felt, and sooner forgotten with them. In general, their existence appears to participate more of sensation than reflection.

... I advance it therefore . . . that the blacks, whether originally a distinct race, or made distinct by time and circumstances, are inferior to the whites in the endowments both of body and mind.

—*Thomas Jefferson, author of the Declaration of Independence and third president of the United States, in* Notes on the State of Virginia, *1781*

Here is [scientific] proof of the necessity of slavery. The African is incapable of self-care and sinks into lunacy under the burden of freedom. It is a mercy to give him the guardianship and protection from mental death.

—*Secretary of State John C. Calhoun, arguing for the extension of slavery, 1844*

Black and other ethnic minority children are uneducable beyond the nearest rudiments of training. No amount of school instruction will ever make them . . . capable citizens. . . . Their dullness seems to be racial, or at least inherent in the family stock from which they come. . . . Children of this group should be segregated in special classes and be given instruction which is concrete and practical. They cannot master abstractions, but they can be made efficient workers. . . . There is no possibility at present of convincing society that they should not be allowed to reproduce, although

from a eugenic point of view they constitute a grave problem because of their unusually prolific breeding.

*—Lewis Terman, Stanford University professor and researcher
and president of the American Psychological Association, in*
The Measurement of Intelligence, *1916*

And more recently:

We now have out there what I call the egalitarian fiction that all
[racial] groups are equal in intelligence. We have social policy
based on that fiction. For example, the 1991 Civil Rights Act . . .
which said that if you have disproportionate hiring by race . . .
that's *prima facie* evidence of racial discrimination. . . . Differences
in intelligence have real world effects, whether we think they're
there or not.

*—Linda Gottfredson, Miller Award for outstanding jour-
nal article, American Psychology Association, 2008; Mensa
Award for Excellence in Research, 2005; quoted from "Race, IQ,
Success and Charles Murray," PBS* Think Tank *transcripts, aired
October 28, 1994*

If you wanted to reduce crime, you could, if that were your sole
purpose, you could abort every black baby in this country and
your crime rate would go down.

*—William Bennett, former secretary of education, on his ra-
dio show,* Morning in America, *2005*

I am gloomy about the prospect of Africa. . . . [Our] social policies

are based on the fact that their intelligence is the same as ours—
whereas all the testing says not really.

—*James Watson, Nobel Prize–winning biologist, 2007*

It would not be difficult to find many more examples. There
is probably no group of people in the world whose intellectual
capacity and innate morality have been so maligned as African
Americans. From the time of enslavement to the present, so-
called scholars have continued to attempt to prove that African
Americans are less intelligent than whites. All of us have been affected by this "scholarship," including, in recent decades, the noto-
rious example of *The Bell Curve*, whose authors received standing
ovations when they spoke in middle-class white communities.

Author Beverly Tatum talks about how people who live in
Los Angeles become smog-breathers. They don't do anything
to become smog-breathers, they aren't conscious of being smog-
breathers, they just go about their everyday lives as they breathe
smog. She then adds that if we live in America, we are racism-
breathers, and it doesn't matter what color we are. We don't try to
be, we aren't usually conscious of the racism we've breathed. We
just go about our regular lives. We are so unconscious of these realities that we seldom see how even our language is embedded with
racist overtones.[9]

Robert Moore wrote a wonderful tongue-in-cheek paragraph,
published in a pamphlet put out by the Council on Interracial
Books for Children, on racism in the English language:

Some may blackly (angrily) accuse him of trying to blacken (de-
fame) the English language, to give it a black eye (a mark of shame)
by writing such black words (hostile). They may denigrate (to cast
aspersions; to darken) him by accusing him of being blackhearted
(malevolent), of having a black outlook (pessimistic, dismal) on

life, of being a blackguard (scoundrel)—which would certainly be a black mark (detrimental fact) against him. Some may blackbrow (scowl at) him and hope that a black cat crosses in front of him because of this black deed. He may become a black sheep (one who causes shame or embarrassment because of deviation from the accepted standards), who will be blackballed (ostracized) by being placed on a blacklist (list of undesirables) in an attempt to blackmail (to force or coerce into a particular action) him to retract his words. But attempts to blackjack (to compel by threat) him will have a Chinaman's chance of success, for he is not a yellow-bellied Indian-giver of words, who will whitewash (cover up or gloss over vices or crimes) a black lie (harmful, inexcusable). He challenges the purity and innocence (white) of the English language. He doesn't see things in black and white (entirely bad or entirely good) terms, for he is a white man (marked by upright firmness) if there ever was one. However, it would be a black day when he would not "call a spade a spade," even though some will suggest a white man calling the English language racist is like the pot calling the kettle black. While many may be niggardly (grudging, scanty) in their support, others will be honest and decent— and to them he says, that's very white of you (honest, decent).[10]

On a more serious note, the larger society seems always ready to identify African Americans with almost all negative behavior. For those who followed the story of Hurricane Katrina, there was the pair of newspaper photos, published at different times, one of which depicted a black survivor with a black plastic bag floating behind him with the caption: "A young man walks through chest-deep flood waters after **looting** a grocery store in New Orleans on Tuesday." In contrast, the second picture showed two white people dragging a bag with the caption, "Two residents wade through chest-deep water after **finding** bread and soda from a local grocery store in New Orleans, Louisiana."[11]

In no way do I believe the caption writers were conscious of the differentiation that was made between black and white people in identical situations, but the racism "smog" that we breathe so often masks unexamined belief systems.

As a result of this "racism smog," many of our children have internalized all of the negative stereotypes inherent in our society's views of black people. A student teacher at Southern University told me that she didn't know what to say when an African American eighth-grade boy came up to her and said, "They made us the slaves because we were dumb, right, Ms. Summers?" Working with a middle schooler on her math, a tutor was admonished, "Why you trying to teach me to multiply, Ms. L.? Black people don't multiply; black people just add and subtract. White people multiply."

When students doubt their own competence, they typically respond with two behaviors: they either hide (hoods over faces, heads on desks) and try to become invisible, or they act out to prevent a scenario unfolding in which they will not be able to perform and will once again be proved "less than." Teachers frequently misinterpret both of these behaviors, usually inferring that the student is unmotivated, uninterested, or behavior disordered. In one classroom I visited, a young third-grade boy was sitting in the back of the class in a corner while the rest of the class worked on a worksheet. The teacher said it was because of misbehavior, but when I asked the boy why he was sitting in the back by himself, he said, "Because I'm dumb." Although the teacher had interpreted the boy's behavior as merely "bad," for the child, his misbehavior was in some way linked to his internalized belief in his "dumbness."

As bad as things are for African Americans in general, African American males present an even more dismal picture. Not only are African American males consistently at the bottom of all educational measures in our schools, the quality of life indicators for African American males suggest that they are in deep trouble in all areas. As Pedro Noguera documents in *The Trouble with Black*

Boys, this group leads the nation in homicides, both as perpetrators and as victims. In an alarming trend, they now have the fastest growing rate of suicide. They have been, for the last several years, contracting HIV/AIDS at a faster rate than any other segment of the population. They are the only group in the United States experiencing a decline in life expectancy. In the labor market, they are the least likely to be hired and, in many cities, the most likely to be unemployed.[12]

There is little doubt that these issues of hardship in the lives of black males affect what happens in schools. Black males are more likely than any other group to be suspended and expelled from schools. After a steady increase in African American enrollment in colleges from 1973 to 1977, since 1977 there has been a sharp and continuous decline, especially among black males. Black males are more likely to be classified as mentally retarded or suffering from a learning or emotional disability and placed in special education. Black males are least likely to be enrolled in advanced placement and honors courses. In contrast to most other groups, where males commonly perform at higher levels in math and science-related courses, the reverse is true for black males. Even class privilege and the material benefits that accompany it fail to inoculate black males from low academic performance: when compared with their white peers, middle-class African American males lag significantly behind in both grade point average (GPA) and standardized-test scores.[13]

In a society that has, in general, stigmatized black males, many of our young men have internalized all of the negative stereotypes. Thus, they are involved in a perfect catch-22. Because of societal stereotypes affecting African American boys, teachers frequently negatively react to normal young black boy behavior. Constant reprimands instill a sense of being "less than" men from a very early age. This perception causes many black males to hide or to act out to protect their sense of self. Their behaviors then reinforce the view of their teachers and others, causing the adults around them to further criticize and marginalize them within the school. This in turn causes the young men to exhibit even more disidentification with school, leading to even more negative attitudes from teachers, more suspensions and expulsions, and so on. Many black males tend to be so alienated from school that they do not feel that the teachers or the setting mean them any good. Research conducted by education Professor Noguera in an academic magnet school (where all the students were selected on the basis of high test scores and GPAs) shows just how alienated from school and their teachers a group of black males felt.

Only 20 percent of the black males interviewed "agreed" or "strongly agreed" with the statement "My teachers support me and care about my success in their class," versus 54 percent of white males and 71 percent of white females. Eighty percent of black males "disagreed" or "strongly disagreed" with the statement. If this is the perceived reality for African American males in a selective magnet school, imagine the level of alienation that our black boys may feel if they are lower performers in traditional academic settings.

The belief of African American children that their teachers are less interested in teaching them may have some support from another line of research. C. Kirabo Jackson, an associate professor of labor economics at Cornell University in Ithaca, New York, studied patterns of teacher movement in Charlotte-Mecklenburg, North Carolina, schools between 2002 and 2003, when the 137,000-student school district ended its long-running policy of busing students to keep schools racially integrated. His results, published in the *Journal of Labor Economics*, show that, at all levels of schooling, high-quality teachers—both black and white—were more likely to switch schools as their current schools gained larger black populations.[14] In other words, for whatever reasons, when black children arrived, some of the best teachers left. What message does that give to African American students and their parents?

African Americans, as well as others who are marginalized by the views of the larger society, are also affected deeply by exposure to the larger society's assumptions of blacks' inferiority when it comes to test performance. Psychologist Claude Steele and his colleagues have researched from the 1990s to the present, what they have termed *stereotype threat*. Stereotype threat is the experience of anxiety or concern in a situation where a person has the potential to confirm a negative stereotype about the social group to which they belong. Steele initially looked at the performance of men and women in a mathematics class, where men typically outperformed women. The group of men and women were given a difficult test in mathematics. Some of the participants were told that men and women typically scored similarly on this particular test and others were told nothing other than that they were taking a test. The participants who were not given instructions showed the expected gender gap in performance—the women scored lower than the men. In contrast, the group that was told that the test did not typically show gender differences displayed no gender-based score differences.

Steele later took a look at black/white testing settings. He and his colleagues administered a difficult language test to black and white college students. One group was told nothing, the other group was told that this was not a diagnostic test, but a tool to see how people already determined to hold strong language skills solved linguistic problems. The first group showed the expected racial gap in performance, with the white students outperforming blacks. In the second group, the gap was eliminated.

Steele and others have found that stereotype threat appears to function in most settings in which a group feels stigma potentially related to its performance. The scores of a group of white men, for example, were lower in one experiment when they were told that a particular test measured natural athletic ability. The scores increased when the stereotype threat was not mentioned, with that group scoring much higher.

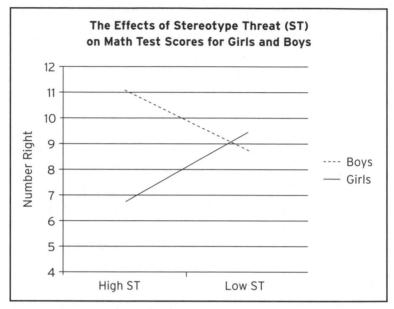

Figure 1. Jason W. Osborne, "Linking Stereotype Threat and Anxiety," *Educational Psychology* 27, no. 1 (2007): 135–54. Reprinted with permission.

As they continued to study the effects of stereotype threat, Steele and his colleagues, as well as other researchers, have uncovered some other interesting findings. In terms of the mechanisms through which stereotype threat affects performance, it has now been shown that settings with high stereotype threat—situations in which participants believe that their performance might support negative stereotypes attributed to the groups to which they belong—are likely to disrupt working memory, increase self-consciousness about one's performance, and cause individuals to try to suppress negative thoughts as well as negative emotions such as anxiety. Physically, heart rate is increased, as is blood pressure.

Another finding is that, ironically, those who are most highly identified with a particular domain (those women who consider

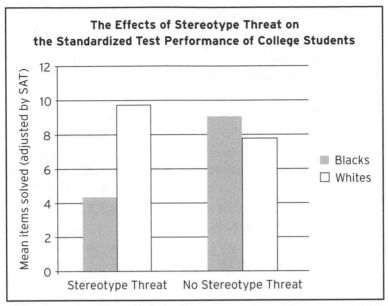

Figure 2. J. Aronson, C.M. Steele, M.F. Salinas, and M.J. Lustina, "The Effect of Stereotype Threat on the Standardized Test Performance of College Students," in *Readings About the Social Animal*, 8th ed., ed. E. Aronson (New York: Freeman).

themselves good mathematicians or those African Americans who see themselves as achievers) are most likely to have their scores depressed by stereotype threat. In other words, caring about the outcome increases the underperformance effect.

A second interesting finding is that over the long term, the chronic experience of stereotype threat appears to lead individuals to "dis-identify" with the domain in which they are experiencing the threat. For example, a woman may stop seeing herself as a "math person," and an African American student may stop believing in his potential to be a scholar. This disidentification may be thought of as a psychological coping strategy that allows an individual to maintain self-esteem in the face of failure. It is not a far reach to suggest that such disidentification is prevalent in many urban schools.[15]

There are a number of strategies the researchers have identified to overcome low performance due to stereotype threat, but they center around creating a sense of belonging for the students—a sense that they belong in the "club" of scholars and achievers; that school is for them.[16] It also involves not putting the students in settings that increase the sense of stereotype stigma. For example, remedial programs may have an unintended side effect of serving to confirm a student's belief in his inability. Rather than identifiable remedial programs, students could be placed in carefully planned accelerated programs that not only ameliorate their lack of preparation but allow them to gain skills that surpass grade or class expectations.

When we attempt to improve achievement in African American students, we must take into consideration not just academic issues but issues of psychological trauma caused by living in a society in which black people have been stigmatized. In one school I visited, students refused to engage in the Read 180 program, put in place to assist students who tested low in reading. The only available room for the program was one that other students passed on their way to lunch. Students assigned to Read 180 felt stigmatized and either refused to come to class or refused to engage. Despite the school's best intentions of providing assistance to those students who were deemed in need of help, it is unlikely that the students showed improvement in the stigmatizing setting.

By contrast, Professor Petra Hendry established a project about ten years ago with students from historically black McKinley High School in Baton Rouge, Louisiana. The students did an oral history project of McKinley, identifying its special history as the first public high school for African Americans in that region. The students were not high performers in school, but they conducted interviews, researched archives, and presented their findings at various venues. In the process of doing the oral history project, they improved reading skills, learned to do archival research, and learned to transcribe tapes (thus practicing punctuation, spelling, etc.). Their work is now in a permanent oral history collection at Louisiana State University. Unlike the Read 180 students, these young people were not cast as dumb, remedial students but as university-affiliated researchers. Which identification would you imagine carries the most psychological potential for having students identify with school and its contents?

The final reason I'd like to propose for why African American students are not achieving at levels commensurate with their ability has to do with curricular content. If the curriculum we use to teach our children does not connect in positive ways to the culture young people bring to school, it is doomed to failure. A wonderful example of a curriculum that connected beautifully with students and their interests was devised at a middle school in Stone Mountain, Georgia, where I spent a year in the 1990s. As in most middle schools around the country, the students were constantly "doing" their own and each other's hair. Every week the teachers would admonish students to stop combing their hair and focus on their education. Every week the students ignored them. In response to the students' near-obsession with their hair, and as an alternative to the endless teacher complaints about this obsession, the school and I made "cosmetological" lemonade: Ok, we'll do hair. The teachers and students explored the mathematics of black hair design, the science of hair product ingredients, hairstyles in every era of ancient and not-so-ancient history, and the multitude of school-based skills necessary to be an effective cosmetologist.

The national Algebra Project, focused on educating those students in the lowest quartile, has based much of its curriculum on students' real life experiences. In the Mississippi Delta the concept of equivalence was approached through the time-tested black cultural notion of "making do." When you don't have an ingredient for biscuits, you "make do" with its equivalent. One boy spoke of having the family car break down because of a broken belt and his father "making do" with an equivalent—his sister's pantyhose! In urban Boston, Algebra Project students learned about numbers also representing directionality (in addition to "amounts") by plotting trips on the subway routes they utilized daily.

In Atlanta, teachers Afiya and Wekesa Madizimoyo got middle school students interested in learning math, economics, marketing, and language arts by having groups of students design sneakers and develop business plans to market their products. They could write the plan focused on an African country—but to choose the best potential marketing site they had to do in-depth studies of each country under consideration. Teacher Rick Ayers's students publish an ever-expanding dictionary of teen language through which they learn about how language changes, how dictionaries are constructed, word derivations, parts of speech, and much of the traditional ELA curriculum. In Louisiana, Derrick Kyle's African American high school students created a feature-length movie, *Drama High*, that was screened at a local theater for family and friends. In the process of creating the film, the students studied literary conventions. They explored plot building, character development, how to create rising action, how to relate subplots, and building and resolving conflict. Mr. Kyle says that the students also became much more conscious of standard language. No amount of teacher correction would have had as much effect in helping students become aware of their use of nonstandard forms than listening to themselves and each other on film. Without the teacher saying one word about it, the students self-corrected orally and became much more careful in their writing.

Louisiana State University professor Sue Weinstein works with a spoken-word project initiated by the Big Buddies Organization in Baton Rouge. In "Wordplay," high school students read, write, and perform their works in citywide competitions. These students meet weekly as they learn to write; practice public speaking and performance; work on grammar, metaphor, written language conventions; and so much more. They read poetry from around the world and so learn about much of the world they may not have the opportunity to see. And they love it. They seek out their teachers to demand editorial assistance. They are engaged. They are learning.

A final example of potentially using children's interests to create curriculum comes from my experiences observing a fifth-grade class in Georgia in the early 2000s. The teacher of the class fully believed that she was teaching social studies and that the students were engaged in learning it. As an observer, I saw something different. The students were definitely engaged—but not in the subject matter the teacher proffered. The fifth graders were fully engaged with each other. They were almost constantly exchanging notes. Many of them had devised such creative methods that the teacher never knew what was happening right under her nose. As they were supposedly writing answers to textbook questions, one would go up to borrow a dictionary, then return the dictionary to the shelf with a note for another student, identified by a brief glance in his or her direction. The addressee would then go up to borrow the same dictionary to secure the note. One of the more remarkable note-passing tricks was to take out the innards of a ball-point pen, roll a note up, and secure it in the pen's barrel. After the pen was "accidentally" dropped on the floor, a quick look determined who should retrieve the pen.

After watching in growing fascination for a few weeks, I retrieved a few discarded notes from the trash can. I asked permission from the three note writers to read and write about their notes. They had no problem giving it. Here is the story I uncovered:

Note 1: Back and forth between Darrell and Catrice:
    D: Girlfreind and boyfriends hold hands. Why don't we?

C: I didn't think you wanted to. I didn't think you wanted to be near me.

Note 2: Back and forth between Darrell and Catrice:

D: alot of Boys say your ugly like Jhon, so I am shie to be around you

C: a lot of Boys are DUMB. All the girls say your ugly But that dose not stop me from likeing you. Just don't lissen to them.

D: if somebody asks if we go out, say no. keep it on the down low.

C: ok

Note 3: (The plot thickens!) From JB to Catrice

JB: Dear Catrice, I know we probably couldn't go together, but I just want to say I like you because your bueatiful, smart, and you have a good sence of humor. So if Darrel dumps you please go with me.

Note 4: From Catrice to Darrell

Dear Darrell,

If people tellyou to dump me

Just don't lissen their just jlous and they want me to go with them.

Love,

Your g/f

Catrice

Note 5: (The dealbreaker) From JB to Catrice

Dear Catrice,

I know you think I'm a freak because I've been acting stupid, but if you could give me one more chance I would treat you like a queen. Every time I look at you my eyes want to ex-

plode with love to you. Can you please give me one more
chance I will never stop liking you.

From JB

Such intense goings on! Needless to say, Catrice ended up—at
least for that week—with JB. (And when I relate the story to my
graduate students I have been asked more than once if JB might
have an older brother!) Clearly, the last thing that the students in
this class had on their minds was the teacher's history lesson. But,
could we garner their interest in love affairs to think about curricular development? What if we developed a history curriculum that
ushered in each era with a focus on a love affair. History provides
endless examples: Napoleon and Josephine, the Trumans, Martin
and Coretta King, King Edward VIII and Wallis Simpson, Hitler
and Eva Braun; Cleopatra, Caesar, and Mark Antony. The list is
endless. Given the propensities of humans, there is no historical
era that would not yield a romantic contribution to curricular design! Perhaps creating such a history curriculum that would be ir-
resistible to middle schoolers will be the next great teacher project.
Any takers?

To conclude, African American students are gifted and brilliant. They do not have a culture of poverty but a culture of rich-
ness that can be brought into classrooms to facilitate learning.
African American students learn when they are taught. They
must be helped to overcome the negative stereotypes about themselves and their communities that permeate our culture. We can
and must build curricula that connect to our students' interests,
thereby allowing them to connect the knowns to the unknowns.
We cannot allow an expectation gap to result in an achievement
gap. Multiplication is for everyone.

2
INFINITE CAPACITY

In eras and locales where the inferiority of African American children has not been presumed, amazing things have happened. Two such examples are in traditional African cultures and another in America during the time of the Civil Rights Movement's Freedom Schools.

I have been informed by studying the traditional African view of education, and I believe that in our American educational world of numbers, reductionism, mechanistic "human-proof" curricula, and robotized interactions, the African worldview could provide our salvation. Asa Hilliard's book *SBA: The Reawakening of the African Mind* includes a discussion of the tenets of traditional African education, involving pedagogical systems that emerged thousands of years ago. Many of the ancient practices still exist in traditional cultures on the African continent and in many places in the African diaspora. Traditional African thought holds that the cosmos is divine and that humans, as part of the cosmos, also have the potential to become divine. The goal of education must be to assist individuals in their quest for divinity or perfection, by fostering a deep understanding and guided practice of the principles of "correct" living.

The aim of traditional African education for the mind is not separated from education for the body. The body was seen as a divine temple, housing a spirit. As a result, the education for mind and body was also linked to education for the spirit. Therefore, in the African tradition, it is the role of the teacher to appeal to the intellect, the humanity, and the spirituality in his or her students. In order to make such an appeal, however, Hilliard and other African-centered scholars remind us, a teacher must be convinced of the inherent intellectual capability, humanity, physical capability, and spiritual character of students.[1]

Pierre Erny tells us in *Childhood and Cosmos* that the search in most African societies is to determine "who" and not "what" the child is, indicating that the child is a unique entity. On the other hand, this very special, divine gift—this child—is also seen in Africa to be a part of a collective, a family, a community. For Africans, the self is incomplete without being incorporated into the larger family. Thus, African traditional education prepared students to work with and be an integral part of a social group. The African saying, "*I* am because *we* are," expresses this sense of connection to and responsibility for the group.[2]

Hilliard cites his interview with Professor Emeh, a traditional healer and university professor from Nigeria, who spoke of the quest in African education to eliminate foolishness.[3] It is foolishness that keeps a person from learning, not the Western notion of mental capacity. Africans assume that people have the mental capacity to achieve, but they are concerned about the "software" that allows brilliant people to misuse the capacity. More often than not, the impediments to learning for Africans are expressed as character deficiencies rather than mental deficiencies, in which case the solution is to motivate the child by whatever means are deemed appropriate to improve his or her attitude. There is no doubt that all humans are *capable* of learning. It would not take much analysis to see the superiority of this kind of thinking to the shallow, numbers-driven farce we inflict upon too many of our children and their teachers on a daily basis.

Interestingly, we have historical precedence in our own country, a time in which poor black students were educated to achieve individual cognitive growth, physical development, spiritual and pragmatic connection to their communities, and where no students were considered to lack the capacity to learn. In the 1960s, when students boycotted or were locked out of Mississippi schools during the Civil Rights Movement, "Freedom Schools" were created by activist teachers and community workers. An archival document produced at the time, a mimeographed page titled "Overview of the Freedom Schools," states:

> The purpose of the Freedom Schools is to create an educational experience for students which will make it possible for them to challenge the myths of our society, to perceive more clearly its realities, and to find alternatives—ultimately new directions for action.... The Freedom Schools will present an intensive curriculum designed to meet several different needs:
>
> An academic curriculum which will . . . sharpen the students' abilities to read, write, work mathematical problems, etc., but will concentrate more on stimulating a student's interest in learning....
>
> The Citizenship curriculum will concentrate on a study of the social institutions which affect students, and the background of the social system which has produced us all at this time. The various sections will be: the Negro in Mississippi, the Negro in the North, Myths about the Negro, the Power Structure, the Poor Negro and the Poor White, Material Things versus Soul Things, and the Movement. In these sections, the student will be encouraged to form opinions about the various social phenomena

which touch him, to learn about his own particular heritage as a Negro, and to explore possible avenues for his future. Special attention at the end of the unit will be devoted to the Civil Rights Movement—the historical development to this point, the philosophical assumptions underlying pressure for social change, and the issues which are currently before the Civil Rights Movement.

Recreational and cultural curriculum, which will be a large part of the day, will try to provide the students with relaxation from their more intensive studies and also an opportunity to express themselves in new ways. The program will include dancing and sports, arts and crafts, dramatics, music, etc.[4]

A First Step Toward Sanity:
Believe in the Children

What can we do today to bring some of the rationality expressed in African traditional thinking and the Freedom Schools of the Civil Rights Movement to the enterprise of educating those children that school systems have typically failed? I believe the first step, as scholars suggest, is to become convinced of these children's inherent intellectual capability, humanity, physical ability, and spiritual character.

Unfortunately, our nation's educational enterprise continues to be obsessed with the notion of intellectual capacity. In a graduate seminar, Hilliard once reminded students that for millions of years, animals and humans have been teaching their young what they need to know to survive. Not one mother tried to find out whether her bear babies or her cat babies or her human babies had the capacity to learn—they just taught them what they needed to know! Over and over we now try to find out what is wrong with the children or their families that stunts their learning, that limits their capacity, without paying sufficient attention to what does or doesn't happen *in classrooms.*

One example that has been cited frequently in reform efforts of the past decade is the study by Betty Hart and Todd Risley. I have no doubts that the study's authors had the best of intentions in pursuing their research. They were led to the study, they say, by struggling unsuccessfully to close the performance gap between poor and middle-class preschool children. Because all of their efforts in preschool were washed out by kindergarten, they conducted the study looking into children's home lives in order to understand why. Their research was conducted over a two-and-a-half-year span and recorded thirty thousand pages of transcripts collected from monthly visits to American families of varied incomes with one- and two-year-old children. The Hart-Risley data concluded that children from low-income families heard many fewer words than children of professional parents and that this disparity in language experience was tightly linked to differences in child outcomes.[5]

They found that a child from a professional family would hear 11 million words during a year while a child in a welfare family would hear just 3 million. Thus, a child from a professional family could start kindergarten having heard 32 million more words than their poorer classmates. As one solution, the authors suggest that there is a need to teach parents and child-care workers to talk more to children of poverty.

It is interesting to think of all the consequences of having heard 43 million words from your parents before kindergarten. I have many highly literate Asian and Native American friends whose traditional cultures tend to dictate much less adult-to-child verbalizations—and who would consider that much talk directed at a child as nothing less than child abuse. I cannot help wondering if these children of "professional families" grow up to be the colleagues at faculty meetings who can take a ten-minute issue and turn it into a three-hour meeting!

The study also reminds me of my own daughter's attempts to stifle my "professional-family" speech to her on numerous occasions. When she was two, I discovered a program called "Potty Training in Less than a Day." The directions indicated that I should let her know every twenty minutes or so about how proud her aunties and uncles, grandmother, various friends, and I would be of her if she were a big girl and used the pot like big girls do. After about six hours of this, I was praising once more. "Maya," I said, "you are such a big girl. Auntie Billie is going to be so proud that you used the pot. Mimi is going to be so very proud that you used the pot. You are so wonderful and such a big girl when you use the pot." She looked at me with two-year-old exasperation and said, "Shub-up, Mommy!"

Then, when she was three, I would regularly do my professional-family language routine in the car: "Maya, do you see those trees? Do you know what color they are? Do you know how they get to be green? The plants grow in the soil and get nutrients and then the sun shines on them and causes them to make a green color. That's called photosynthesis. Can you say that big word? . . . etc." My child looked at me and said with great firmness, "Mommy, get out of my mind!" And so, I came to understand that part of raising a sane child is allowing her to have her own thinking time, not always being bombarded with adult language.

And, with respect to the study, I can only imagine how a professional family would act when being observed for language use by a researcher. Like most of us, the parents would tend to talk more to show how well they interact with their children. I can also imagine how a poor family would react. The parents might very possibly talk *less* so as not to say things that they thought might be embarrassing.

But, even if the research is completely accurate—and I have no evidence to doubt its accuracy—the reality is that no matter how much language the parents do or don't use with their children, appropriate instruction in school can resolve the problem. But the solution cannot be some "quick fix" initiated only in preschool or kindergarten; it must be a continued effort that involves a completely different kind of instruction. Educators have proven this over and over again. Black teachers in the pre-integration South regularly educated children of poverty to levels that allowed them to enter universities successfully and indeed to become local and national leaders no matter how many words their parents spoke to them as toddlers. More recently, the Marcus Garvey School in Los Angeles, California; the Chick School in Kansas City, Missouri; Harmony-Leland in Cobb County, Georgia; and the Prescott School in Oakland, California, among many others, have all educated low-income African American children who have performed at higher levels on mandated standardized tests than even some of the schools serving the most affluent students in their respective districts.[6] Sankofa Shule, a public, African-centered, charter school in Lansing, Michigan, produced low-income African American students who read two to four levels above grade level, who did algebra and calculus in grade school, and who outscored the Lansing School District and the state of Michigan on the state accountability test (MEAP) in 2000 in mathematics and writing. The school was called "an educational powerhouse" by *U.S. News & World Report* in the April 27, 1998, issue. The principal who led that school later took on a low-performing regular public school in Michigan with similar results.[7]

These educational institutions and individual teachers realize that there is no preschool "vaccination" that can help poor children, who do not have access to the culture of power to be successful in later school years. Only a consciously devised, continuous program that develops vocabulary in the context of real experiences, provides rigorous instruction, connects new information to the cultural frameworks that children bring to school, and assumes that the children are brilliant and capable—and teaches accordingly—can. Examples of this kind of instruction will be described in later chapters.

A Second Step Toward Sanity:
"Fight Foolishness"

The second task we must accomplish if we wish truly to educate the children we have heretofore failed is, in the words of Professor Emeh, to "fight foolishness."[8] Or, as educator Herb Kohl says in his book *Stupidity and Tears*, to "fight stupidity."[9] We have to cease attempting to build "teacher-proof" schools with scripted low-level instruction and instead seek to develop (and retain) perceptive, thinking teachers who challenge their students with high-quality, interactive, and thoughtful instruction.

Now a principal, then a teacher, Paula White-Bradley described how her former school required teachers to enact the *Success for All* reading block. During this time, the students were supposed to work in teams. Teachers were instructed to "manage" the teams by awarding team points for students' behavior, including getting along together, collectively participating, and completing tasks. The group work was to be painstakingly timed by the teacher, regardless of the amount of time actually needed for students to complete the tasks. Therefore, teams were typically awarded points for nonacademic tasks such as being the first to stack their books in the center of the table or being the first to transition quickly from one activity to the next. Each team was to begin the reading period with zero points. They were then to work their way up to "earning" a maximum of twenty points. Thus, much of both the students' and the teacher's time was spent on "housekeeping" tasks related to keeping order, with no time for deep discussion about anything the children (or teachers) wanted to explore. Furthermore, the classrooms were monitored by the program's consultants—popularly known among the teachers as "the *Success for All* police"—whose work was to ensure that all the rules were followed exactly.[10] Unfortunately, many classrooms in our country are still confined by this and other educational programs that require similar thoughtless regimentation.

If we want children from low-income families to achieve at high levels, this kind of instruction can only be construed as "foolishness." To expend so much of a teacher's energy on keeping track of "points" related to noninstructional tasks, and to prevent any kind of deep instruction about what is being studied, can lead only to the lowest level of academic development. This is the reason we *never* see these prepackaged "teacher-proofed" programs in affluent schools, only in schools serving low-income children and children of color.

Kohl quotes Jules Henry on the issue of sanity:

> Sanity . . . can take three forms—to believe sham to be the truth; to see through sham while using it; or to see through sham but fight it. . . . We are now in the stage of believing sham to be the truth, while entering the stage of seeing through sham while using it. The third stage is understanding sham and knowing how to fight it. The fourth stage is a world without sham.[11]

It will likely be a while before we get there. We are still managing to waste poor children's time on activities that have no real relationship to intellectual development. We are still driving great, creative teachers out of the field by proscribing their efforts to bring challenging, meaningful instruction to their charges. Kohl rightly says that the sham, the stupidity, is disheartening, but perhaps it can also be a call to resistance and the rebirth of teacher—and let's hope researcher—militancy. Rather than spending time on such "foolishness," what teachers should be doing is developing the knowledge of the outside world that children from less privileged families might lack.

*   *   *

What those who have been successful teaching these children to achieve at high levels know is that they do not need to "fix" the language of the parents, or to devise some preschool intervention that will "fix" the children, or to "dumb-down" teaching with scripted instruction. Rather, students need focused instructional strategies throughout their school years that are designed specifically for their cultural and academic backgrounds.

The "fourth grade slump" that poor children encounter in schools is well documented.[12] When students reach fourth grade and are required to "read to learn" rather than "learn to read," they need considerable vocabulary and background knowledge to make sense of required reading material in classrooms and on standardized tests. If their earlier school years have not focused on developing knowledge about the world outside of their environs or deep thinking about real issues, they are destined to fall behind.

In my work observing dozens of successful classrooms, effective teachers of low-income students of color take every opportunity to introduce children to complex material. While children are learning to "decode," teachers read to the children complex, thought-provoking material, well above the students' current reading level and engage in discussions about the information and the advanced vocabulary they encounter. Students are involved in activities that use the information and vocabulary in both creative and analytical ways, and teachers help them create metaphors for the new knowledge that connects this knowledge to the students' lives. Students memorize and dramatize material that involves advanced vocabulary and linguistic forms. Students are engaged in thematic units that are ongoing and repeat important domain knowledge and develop vocabulary through repeated oral use. In these successful classrooms, students are also asked to explain what they have learned to others, thus solidifying new knowledge. For example, I recently visited Ms. Seals's class of African American first graders who could discern and label fiction, nonfiction, realistic fiction, and other literary genres. They used this knowledge as they discussed each other's writing and offered editing suggestions.

Researchers have documented the efficacies of these expanded teaching strategies.[13] Successful instruction is constant, rigorous, integrated across disciplines, connected to students' lived cultures, connected to their intellectual legacies, engaging, and designed for critical thinking and problem solving that is useful beyond the classroom. Never do the successful teachers of these children believe that students have learned enough or that they cannot learn more.

Make no mistake, when we fail to provide such instruction, when we fail to educate children in inner-city schools, the students are quite aware of our failures to teach them. Despite their purposeful attempts to "not learn," as Kohl calls it—enlisting various forms of classroom disruption and disengagement to thwart the system that disrespects them and assumes their intellectual inferiority—they are saddened and, indeed, brokenhearted with the results.

Kohl introduces us to one youngster who became ever more frustrated with his continuing school failure and the lack of support from the school. Instead of putting forth what he determined was useless effort, Reginald declared, "I'd rather be defiant and stupid in class than let the teacher call me a failure. My friends know I'm not dumb and we laugh at the teacher together."[14] It is not hard to hear the hurt in his words, nor to imagine the devastating consequences of this attempt to cope.

A Third Step Toward Sanity: Learn Who Our Children Are and Discover the Legacies They Bring

The third element we must incorporate into our educational system if we are truly to educate poor African American children is that we must learn *who* the children are and not focus on *what* we assume them to be—at risk, learning disabled, unmotivated, defiant, behavior disordered, etc. This means developing relationships with our students and understanding their political, cultural, and intellectual legacy.

Despite some of the beliefs of today's scholars and the general public—black *and* white—people of African descent have an exceptionally long history of educational excellence. In my continuing, but still elementary, study of African history, I have learned that there were centers of higher education in Africa long before European penetration into the continent. From the major centers of higher education in Timbuktu and Mali, to the Sokoto Empire in Nigeria and the Congo, African peoples developed the earliest of advanced educational systems. Education remained a valued commodity during and subsequent to African enslavement. Enslaved Africans risked life and limb to learn to read and write the English language. After legal enslavement ended, the first goal in African American communities was to create schools.

In the history of this country, as Theresa Perry points out in *Young, Gifted and Black*, African Americans pursued educational achievement with a vengeance, and for its own inherent rewards, even though there was no expectation of benefiting from advanced education in the same ways that whites did in the larger society.[15] She poses several interesting questions: Why should one make an effort to excel in school if one cannot determine whether the learning will ever be valued, seen, or acknowledged? Why should one focus on learning in school if that learning will not affect, inform, or alter one's status as a member of an oppressed group? She looks to Jim Anderson, historian of African American education, to find an answer from African Americans themselves and concludes, "For African Americans, from slavery to the modern Civil Rights Movement, the answers were these: You pursued learning because this is how you asserted yourself as a free person; how you claimed your humanity. You pursued learning so you could work for social uplift, for the liberation of your people. You pursued education so you could prepare yourself to lead your people."[16, 17] These answers are a far cry from the one we give our children today—to get a job.

In an attempt to develop a theory of black achievement, Perry offers an analysis of why educational attainment was such a clear goal for African Americans in the past and why that goal has become so much murkier in today's society. From the period of African enslavement until America's present, the dominant belief system has disparaged the academic competence, even the academic capacity, of African Americans. This belief system has sometimes been related as genetic inferiority, more recently as "the culture of poverty," and even more recently, as a dearth of spoken words. This is and was the ideology of white supremacy, most overtly visible in Jim Crow and the pre–Civil Rights era. Historically, black institutions organized themselves to counter this hegemonic belief. In Perry's words:

> Most if not all of the historically Black segregated schools that African-American children attended were intentionally organized in opposition to the ideology of Black inferiority. In other words, in addition to being sites of learning, they also instituted practices and expected behaviors and outcomes that not only promoted education—an act of insurgency in its own right—but also were designed to counter the ideology of African Americans' intellectual inferiority and ideologies that saw African Americans as not quite equal and as less than human. Everything about these institutions was supposed to affirm Black humanity, Black intelligence, and Black achievement.[18]

In black schools, churches, clubs—indeed, all black community institutions—everything focused on this one goal. In all settings there were intentional activities and opaque belief systems designed to ensure achievement, as well as rituals including uplifting songs, recitations, and performances. High expectations, extensive academic support in and out of school, and regular assemblies of students to express the expectations of the adults around them that they must work hard to be free, were also features of these institutions.

Perry uses the example of the graduation described by Maya Angelou in her autobiographical novel *I Know Why the Caged Bird Sings:* The entire community participated in the upcoming ceremony in Stamps, Arkansas. The students built sets, prepared dramatic readings, and practiced songs. There was a celebratory buzz as the community not only acknowledged individuals' accomplishments but reaffirmed the entire community's commitment to academic achievement.

The graduation was to begin with the traditional opening sequence used in the black community—the singing of the national anthem, the recitation of the Pledge of Allegiance, and the singing of the black national anthem. After the pledge, however, two white male representatives from the county interrupted the ceremony. One of the white men came to the stage, ostensibly to bring greetings and congratulations to the graduates, but his words actually carried a very different message. He spoke of the wonderful changes in store for the children of Stamps. He reported that a well-known artist was coming to teach art to the children at the "white school," and that he often bragged on the athletic prowess of the children at the "colored" school. In Angelou's own words,

> The white kids were going to have a chance to be the Galileos and Madame Curies and Edisons and Gauguins, and our boys (the girls weren't even in on it) would try to be Jessie Owenses and Joe Louises. . . . Graduation, the hush-hush magic time of thrills and gifts and congratulations and diplomas, was finished for me be-

fore my name was called. The accomplishment was nothing. The meticulous maps drawn in three colors of ink, learning and spelling decasyllabic words, memorizing the whole of "The Rape of Lucrece"—it was for nothing. Donleavy [the white speaker] had exposed us. . . . We were the maids and farmers, handymen and washerwomen, and anything higher that we aspired to was farcical and presumptuous.[19]

Angelou wrote of how the sense of ugliness that followed Donleavy's remarks was palpable, how she and others were left deflated even after the singing of "Onward Christian Soldiers" and the recitation of William Ernest Henley's poem "Invictus." She provided a window into her own thoughts of hopelessness, even as the valedictorian completed his address, "To Be or Not to Be": "Hadn't he got the message? There was no 'nobler in the mind' for Negroes, because the world didn't think we had minds, and they let us know it."[20]

But then, as soon as Henry Reed, the valedictorian, finished his speech, he turned to face the graduating class on stage and led them and the entire community in the singing of the black national anthem that had been interrupted by the white visitors:

Lift every voice and sing
Till earth and heaven ring
Ring with the harmonies of liberty
Stony the road we trod
Bitter the chastening rod
Felt I the days when hope, unborn, had died
Yet with a steady beat
Have not our weary feet
Come to the place for which our fathers sighed?[21]

After the ritual of collectively singing the black national anthem, the community reminded itself of its focus on "education as an act of freedom, as an act of resistance, as a political and communal act."[22] After that collective gesture, Angelou recalls that the community was "on top again. . . . The depths had been icy and dark, but now bright sun spoke to our souls. I was no longer simply a member of the proud graduating class of 1940; I was a proud member of the wonderful, beautiful Negro race."[23]

Educational achievement was not just for the white world, but for our own community, our own pride. It was for something greater than oneself. Achievement was, as in traditional African belief systems, a reach for the divine, it was about ensuring that the individual was socialized as an integral part of the community family and that everyone in the family was groomed to develop, in Perry's words, an "identity of achievement."[24]

Today's schools, integrated or not, are seldom these kinds of intentional communities. In the post–Civil Rights era, most public schools are deritualized institutions. Certainly, they are not institutions that are intentionally organized to counter inferiority myths. And because of the lack of that kind of institutional space, black students today, as perhaps never before, are victims of the myths of inferiority and find much less support for countering these myths and embracing academic achievement outside of individual families than at other times in the past.

Many years ago, my nephew shocked me. He was in high school, and although I was only six years his senior, because of that age difference I had spent the majority of my school years in segregated, black-run institutions, where my classmates and I had been drilled in the "intentional community" of achievement: "You have to be twice as good as white kids if you want to go half as far," and "your ancestors sacrificed too much for you not to do your best." He, on the other hand, had spent most of his school years in newly integrated settings. I was berating him for making a "D" in chemistry. His response was, "Well, what do you expect from me, the *white* kids get Cs!" His integrated schooling, without the collective support of the African American cultural belief in black potential, had quickly damaged his belief in the ability of people who looked like him to achieve.

Part of truly honing the genius of our children would be consciously to organize institutions and instruction inside and outside of school buildings that expose the children to their intellectual legacy; clarify their position in a racialized society; ritually express expectations for hard work and academic, social, physical, and moral excellence; and create alternative reasons for success other than "getting a good job"—for your community, for your ancestors, for your descendants.

In her most recent book, *In Search of Wholeness*, educator Jackie Irvine writes collaboratively with successful African American teachers of children of color and graduate students who observe and interview the teachers.[25] Irvine summarizes the book's findings by pointing out that the African American teachers whom she studied not only viewed teaching as telling, guiding, and facilitating mastery of mandated content standards but also defined teaching as a calling, not a job. (A friend and colleague, George Vilson, who teaches in a low-income area of Brooklyn, once told me that he has to consider teaching a calling because "they don't pay me enough to consider it a job!") Irvine's teachers conceived of their jobs as "othermothering," caring, believing, demanding the best, and providing the discipline to succeed in life, all reflections of those elements that would be included in the traditional African model.[26]

What Excellence Might Look Like

One of the best examples of the kind of teaching I refer to is embodied in now-retired Oakland, California, elementary school teacher, Carrie Secret. Carrie's students were consistently among the top scorers on district-wide tests, outperforming those in many more-affluent schools. Carrie used both the lived culture and the intellectual legacy of the African American students she taught. She provided a rigorous curriculum. She spoke of each of her charges as spiritual beings, whose spirits she had the honor of nurturing. Hilliard describes her classroom:

> In public performances, the children . . . present spirited inter-
> pretive renderings of great African literature, the poetry of Ilyana
> Vansant [sic] . . . the thirty-four-hundred-year-old Egyptian teach-
> ings of Ptahhotep, creative essays researched and written by Secret,
> among other writings. The short public presentations cannot cap-
> ture the essence of the hours of study that the teacher and students
> must do in preparation. Students are not permitted merely to do
> rote presentations.
>
> To visit Carrie Secret's class is to enter a truly intellectual
> world—and a very spiritual one as well. The walls are covered with
> charts, art, and short selections of masterpieces of literature. . . .
> The faces are predominantly African; however, a child of any eth-
> nic background is honored by having the whole class learn about
> his or her cultural background. These materials are incorporated
> seamlessly into the regular classroom work in all disciplines. . . .
> Secret's children engage in the classroom in critical analysis and
> commentary on [serious, culturally significant] matters. . . . Secret's
> classes are full of movement and action, much of it collective. The
> children sing and dance to serious themes. They do art and write
> stories and essays. . . . All of these things are for a purpose.[27]

Secret read from African and African American texts too difficult for elementary students to decode, as she developed their understanding of themselves and their people. Thus they learned new
grammatical structures, vocabulary, and the use of sophisticated
literary forms not often present in materials simple enough for primary students to decode.

In one series of lessons, she had third graders re-create a sermon of famous minister Jeremiah Wright as a dramatic performance. The sermon was not written for children and was full of difficult vocabulary and complex metaphorical allusions. She and the children defined the vocabulary together, delved into the metaphors, and explored the meaning of each line of the often complicated text. The students wrote about how the text connected to their own lives, and they explored how the messages in the sermon connected to other literature they had studied. Only after exhaustive analysis, did the children then "perform" the text for parents and for other adults. I have seen one of their performances and know firsthand why they routinely move their audiences to standing ovations, shouts of approval, and tears of pride. These children knew what they were talking about, knew what it meant to them, and knew how to make others believe it.

Secret also taught mathematics, social studies, values, and instructional independence (children worked all afternoon on independent individual and collective projects) in the context of traditional African methodologies. She never assumed there was a child who could not learn. Many of her students were labeled as needing special education, but when she treated them as scholars, they behaved like scholars. Indeed, she once told a group of my graduate students that so-called crack babies were only difficult because they were so smart and so fast. She said that their brains work so fast that we are just unable to keep up with them. When we can think nearly as fast as they do, we can learn to teach them.[28]

Before Paula White-Bradley moved to the aforementioned school monitored by the *Success for All* police, she worked in a school that allowed teachers more latitude in their instructional choices. Paula was the seventh-grade social studies teacher, and I was a curriculum consultant at the school. Based on our work together, we collaborated on an article about culturally based behavior management. In this article we explored the use of African content and principles to engage students and to create a family classroom setting. While teaching world history, Paula delved into one of the most studied and admired civilizations in history—ancient Egypt, or Kemet, as it was known to the people of that region.

As the students and teacher explored this classical civilization, the students, all African American, became fascinated with its intricacies. They were even more intrigued by the images of the Kemetic people, photographs of actual statues, and paintings collected from friends who had visited Egypt and not from U.S. sources. "That man look just like my Uncle Jimmy," declared one student with dark brown skin. "How come they're so black? They don't look like the people in *The Mummy*," questioned another. Once the students realized that the Kemetic people of the most significant historical periods looked like the people they thought of as African, indeed looked similar to themselves, they found their studies even more intriguing.

Paula channeled this interest into a study of the Ma'at value system, an all-encompassing system of seven principles that composed the moral system of Kemet. These principles are *truth, justice, harmony, balance, order, reciprocity,* and *righteousness.* The class studied Ma'at by engaging in many oral and written discussions about the principles. They explored the overarching African notion of the responsibility of the individual to the group—"I am because we are." They discussed the need to make their classroom like a family. The students then made a Ma'at quilt in which they created visual interpretations of the meaning of each principle. For example, one student drew a picture of a scale to represent balance and one drew a group engaged in a roundtable discussion to represent justice. In all, over thirty quilt pieces were created, mounted on chart paper, and displayed on the wall as a representation of their understanding of Ma'at.

But the unit did not end with a theoretical understanding of

Figure 3. A pillar of the Egyptian deity Osiris in the image of Senusret I, Pharaoh of Egypt from 1971 BC to 1926 BC. Photograph courtesy of Araldo De Luca.

the concepts. During the course of the study, students engaged in many discussions about the use of Ma'at principles in their classroom and in their everyday lives. They also began to use Ma'at in the classroom to resolve disputes. In one classroom episode, a boy took a girl's pencil. Instead of her usual physical response to the transgression, she looked at the Ma'at quilt and asked him what kind of reciprocity that was. "Would you want me to do that to you?" The boy sheepishly returned the pencil.

An even greater challenge came when a girl transferred into the classroom from another school. In that school she had been placed in a self-contained "behavior disordered" classroom. Shanice challenged the now orderly classroom on her first day, playing her Walkman, singing aloud to explicit lyrics, and making reference to the vernacular word for "whore" when the class discussed hoes and other tools used in agriculture in ancient civilizations. When some members of the class laughed, Shanice felt she had achieved a captive audience and proceeded to ignore the teacher's directives and use increasingly vulgar language, even chronicling her supposed sexual exploits of the night before. Even after Paula talked privately to Shanice and told her of the inappropriateness of her behavior and the plan to contact her mother later that day, Shanice's behavior remained unchanged.

By this time, both the students and the teacher had begun to lose patience with Shanice's outbursts and decided to invoke the ultimate response to an individual's behavior when it endangered the group. The class collectively progressed to the last level of behavioral consequence—the offender is deemed temporarily "out of the family." For the remainder of the class period the student is ignored, no questions or comments elicit a response, no joke is laughed at, no actions acknowledged. The student has the opportunity later to process the incident with the teacher in order to prevent future incidents, and more importantly, the conversation is undertaken in a manner that allows the teacher to connect with the student's spirit in a deep and intimate way. In Shanice's case, the intervention was successful because of the teacher's willingness to build a relationship with her and because of her classmates' willingness to respect the integrity of the "family" and disengage from her behavior without malice. There were certainly additional challenges, but these were undertaken with Shanice as a *participating member* of the classroom rather than as an outside agitator.

We *can* educate all children if we truly want to. To do so, we must first stop attempting to quantify their capacity. We must be convinced of their inherent intellectual capability, humanity, and spiritual character. We must fight the foolishness proliferated by those who believe that one number can measure the worth and drive the education of human beings or that predetermined scripts can make for good teaching. Finally, we must learn *who* our children are—their lived cultures; their interests; and their intellectual, political, and historical legacies. Like Carrie Secret, we must create Perry's "intentional communities," designed around a counter-narrative—one that affirms black brilliance both to the students themselves and to their communities. Like Paula White-Bradley, we must call upon the connections to their heritage to touch the spirits of the children we meet.

Then we can support our students' and our own quest for divinity. Then we can begin to educate the inheritors of the planet.

PART TWO
EDUCATING THE YOUNGEST

3

STUFF YOU NEVER WOULD SAY:
SUCCESSFUL LITERACY INSTRUCTION
IN ELEMENTARY CLASSROOMS

If we are going to ensure that all children learn to read, I believe we have to turn our notion of "basic skills" on its head. What we call "basic skills" in literacy are typically the linguistic *conventions* of middle-class society and the *strategies* successful people use to access new information. For example, punctuation, grammar, specialized subject vocabulary, mathematical operations, five-paragraph essays, and so forth, are all conventions. Using phonetic cues to read words, knowing how to solve word problems, determining an author's purpose, and finding meaning in context are all strategies. All children need to know these things. Some learn them from being read to at home. Some learn them writing thank you notes for their birthday presents under their parents' tutelage. Some learn them just living in a middle-class home environment. What we call basic skills are only "basic" because they are one aspect of the cultural capital of the middle class.

What we call advanced or higher-order skills—analyzing new information, synthesizing disparate concepts, and evaluating the relative merits of concepts—are those that middle-class children learn later in life; yet many children from low-income families learn them much earlier. We of the middle class tend to infantilize our children more than other cultures do. Bonnie, a friend and former graduate student, taught kindergarten in an Alaskan village where the Native Alaskan families had considerably less income than white town families. She then came to teach in town, where most of her kindergarten students were white and middle class. While the town children scored high on all the readiness tests of "basic skills," Bonnie still exclaimed to me one day, "My God, these [town] kids don't know anything! They don't even know how to tie their shoes." Of course, for a kindergarten teacher, tying shoes is a big issue. She also meant that, unlike her village kids, her town students were not able to work independently or to solve any of the typical classroom dilemmas (spilled paint, lost jackets, disputed pencils, etc.) without her direct intervention.

Middle-class parents do a lot for their children, so those children don't often develop real-life problem-solving skills at the rate of those whose parents value independence more. Thus, our middle-class children often don't learn what we refer to as higher-order thinking skills until later. Instead, we parents are busy teaching them "basic skills" like letter-sound correspondences, book language, and how to manipulate numbers. We're also protecting them from life's challenges, solving their problems, and tying their shoes.

Learning at Home and at School

My point is that children come to us having learned different things in their four-to-five years at home. For those who come to us knowing how to count to one hundred and to read, we need to teach them problem solving and how to tie their shoes. And for those who already know how to clean up spilled paint, tie their shoes, prepare meals, and comfort a crying sibling, we need to make sure that we teach them the school knowledge that they haven't learned at home. Unfortunately, though, different types of skills are not equally valued in the school setting.

Because middle-class home culture is so taken for granted, so "transparent," it often exists outside of conscious awareness for those who are members of that culture, especially in schools. It is assumed to be what "everyone knows," just the background of normal life—knowledge that does not need to be taught. Consequently, when this knowledge is not exhibited by children or adults, there is a sense that something is wrong, perhaps a lack of basic intelligence.

When many look at low-income children of color in low-performing schools, they identify what the children don't know—much of it the vocabulary, strategies, or conventions of middle-class life. None of the early school assessments look at what these children *do* know—how to make accurate judgments and evaluate real-life situations accurately and act accordingly. When they don't see evidence of what they believe to be "basic skills," schools frequently judge the students and their families, rather than the instruction, as deficient. Many children are then recommended for special education placement or placed in remedial programs based on instruction in isolated, decontextualized skills—programs that still do not have the capacity to provide them with the nuanced information they have not acquired about middle-class norms. This is not what children need, or how people learn best. "Basic skills"—knowledge of the strategies and conventions of middle-class cultural capital—can and must definitely be taught, but are best taught and learned within the context of meaningful, engaging instruction.

Theresa Perry describes a scenario of an African American third grader who has been enrolled in a city-to-suburb busing program since kindergarten. The girl's teacher in the predominantly white school tells the child's mother that she thinks her daughter might need to be assessed for special education placement. The child is assessed, and contrary to the teacher's expectations, scores above grade level. When the parent talks to the teacher she is told that the teacher is concerned that the child does not know what a canoe is. The mother informs her that the child does know what a boat is. The teacher then says that the child doesn't know what a polliwog is. The mother says she doesn't either and asks what it is. When the teacher tells her that it is a tadpole, the mother says that the child knows what a tadpole is.

Perry comments that although the child is being judged by what she does not know, the school, in her three years there, had done little to help her acquire the knowledge on which she would be eventually judged. Instead of merely teaching that which middle-class children learn at home, we educators too often assume there is something deficient in low-income children or their families that stunts learning. We fail to pay sufficient attention to what we can control—what does or doesn't happen *in classrooms*.

By contrast, Perry cites a teacher in another school who introduced her early elementary students to a unit she developed on the interaction between Asians and Africans along the Silk Road. As a part of this information-rich, exciting, hands-on unit, she and her students talked about transportation by water and the range of vessels that made such transportation possible. Their "word wall" listed words for all kinds of boats—tugboat, sailboat, canoe, and whale boat, as well as words for parts of the boats. This teacher, aware that her inner-city students had not likely had much experience with boats, took the opportunity to provide for them the cultural capital provided by many middle-class homes. She did not make a negative assessment of her students' ability based on their lack of knowledge of middle-class vocabulary. She just taught what they needed to know in an exciting context.[1]

When my daughter Maya was two years old, I was entranced by her every utterance. When she began singing around the house one day, "M-m-m-Maya," I immediately picked up her chant with "Yes, and m-m-m-mommy and m-m-m-milk!" I ushered her to the refrigerator magnets to show her the "m" and showed her how to spell her name. By the time she entered school, she knew all of her letters and letter sounds, although I had never introduced one worksheet into our interactions. I am sure that her teacher thought she taught Maya how to read, but the reality was that Maya, like many middle-class children, had learned most of what she knew about literacy at home. Her kindergarten teacher put her in the "high" group, while those children whose parents had not focused on letters and sounds in the same way that I had were put into a lower group. Those children were in no way less intelligent or less capable of learning. They had just not come to school already knowing what the teacher was supposed to be teaching. Yet, they were already identified as "slow," even before they were ever taught.

Successful teachers of children marginalized either by income-level or ethnicity—or both—have long understood that their charges not only need strong instruction in skills, but they need to know that it is skills, and not intelligence, that they lack. In a case study of four teachers who exhibit powerful pedagogy for African American students, Tyrone Howard cites "Hazel" who believes that many of her students do not fare well academically because they perceive themselves to have insufficient levels of "smartness." They believe that some individuals have smartness and others do not. Consequently, a major part of Hazel's skill development was to stress to her students that all people are smart, but that some of them have different skill levels. Skills, she would insist, are something that you develop over time. If some other individuals appeared smarter, it was because they put forth the effort and made the necessary sacrifices to increase their skills. To quote this wise teacher at length:

> You see, [students] compare themselves to their [classmates] and they say, "Yeah, he's smart, and I'm dumb." So they have this idea

of innate intelligence; even though they don't have the words to explain it, this is what they believe. . . . A lot of [self-doubting] occurs from what other teachers have told them or how they've treated them. . . . [Initially,] I didn't know how to overcome that [type of thinking]. I kept saying, "But you can do this, you can do this," and they kept looking at me like I had lost my ever-loving mind, looking at me like, "She just don't know that I'm stupid." . . . So I talked to them about developing *strategies* and building *skills* that can help them become smart [italics added].[2]

There are numerous schools around the country today that have educated low-income African American children to perform higher on standardized tests than many of the schools serving the most affluent students in their respective districts.[3] These educational institutions and individually successful teachers realize that there is no preschool "vaccination" that will help poor children who do not have access to the culture of power to be successful in later school years. It is not as if middle-class families stop providing cultural capital to their children after kindergarten so that low-income children who "caught up" in kindergarten would then be on a level playing field.

But again, I do not advocate that skills be taught through a steady diet of isolated, fill-in-the-blank worksheets. Only a consciously devised, continuous program that teaches skills and develops vocabulary in the context of real experiences, provides rigorous instruction, connects new information to the cultural frameworks that children bring to school, and assumes that the children are brilliant and capable—and teaches accordingly—can. We cannot successfully teach the necessary vocabulary, strategies, and conventions by depending on the presentation of isolated bits of information and expect children to learn the subtle shadings necessary for communicative competence in this society. Focusing solely on the minutiae of learning will not create educated people.

But that is exactly what is happening too often, in too many of our schools.

One evening more than a decade ago, when my daughter was in first grade, she had a homework assignment to write three sentences, much like so many of the homework assignments I still see today. She was a child who loved to write, so I didn't anticipate any problems with the assignment. We discussed topics she could write about—her grandmother's upcoming visit, her recent birthday party, or the antics of her two new kittens. As she began to write, the telephone rang, and I walked away to answer it. After finishing the phone call, I came back to see how she was doing. She informed me that she was finished and gave me her notebook to read what she had written: "The dog can run. The boy is tall. The man is fat." I was puzzled by the lack of any personal significance in her words, and finally responded, "That's really great, Maya, but what happened to writing about your grandmother or the party or the kittens?" My six-year-old looked patiently at me and said with great deliberateness, "But Mom, I'm supposed to write *sentences!*" Still trying to get a handle on her perspective, I asked, "Maya, what are sentences?" She responded quickly, "Oh, you know, Mom, stuff you write, but you never would say." Ah, so.

This teacher had, I'm sure inadvertently, taught that sentences were meaningless, decontextualized statements you find in workbooks and on the blackboard that "you never would say." Written work in school was not connected to anything real, certainly not to real language. As all good, experienced teachers know, there are many ways to make school feel like it is a part of real life. Spelling words can be taken from stories children write in invented spelling. Grammar conventions can be taught as they arise in the letters children can write to their sports heroes or the plays they might write to perform for the class. Strategies can be taught in the context of solving community problems, building model rockets, reading or writing the directions for new board games, or learning to summarize and simplify a concept into a form appropriate for teaching to a younger child. Strategies and conventions must be taught, but they must be taught within contexts that provide meaning.

I have never presented myself as a reading researcher, only as a teacher who has "taught" reading. (I hesitate to use this term because I believe that rather than teach children to read, we instead give them opportunities to learn how.) Yet, the more I explore research on reading, the more I realize that I understand our limited knowledge of what actually transpires during the learning-to-read process. First, I don't believe any of us knows how a child actually learns to read. Given the differences in the ways our students approach almost everything, there should be little doubt that different children latch onto different features of text to make their first inroads into literacy. Some will connect letters and sounds, some are so sensitive to the way language works that they will focus on meaning and learn to expect some words to follow each other, and some will connect meaning to the shape of a word. Many will probably do some of all three or figure out another path into decoding. My point is that even though teachers have the wonderful opportunity to see something click as their students crack the code of reading, we don't know *what* clicked. Thus, most successful teachers watch what their students are doing and try to expose them to as many tools as possible to map language onto text.

A Political Aside

One big dilemma in reading instruction is that teachers are often prevented from engaging in this kind of skills instruction by mandates demanded by particular reading programs. I have now lived long enough to understand the persistence of a national or regional pendulum swinging to some newly hyped published program that promises to magically transform all students into readers without the teachers having to do anything but recite a printed script. Unlike successful teachers who preferably start with their students' needs and present a variety of decoding and comprehension strategies, the pendulum swings tend to focus on one or another set of strategies to the exclusion of others. This problem has been exacerbated by the newfound omnipresence of governmental policy makers and their cronies in the instructional arena.

The federally funded *Reading First* program is a clear example of inappropriate governmental interference and fiscal misconduct in education. *Reading First* was launched by the No Child Left Behind Act in 2002. States could receive federal funds for reading instruction only if they chose to adopt one of the legislation's "approved" reading programs for its struggling readers. The programs were supposed to be "research based," but even members of the National Reading Panel—who authored the report on the basis of which the programs were supposedly selected—expressed "grave concerns" about the recommended reading programs. A heavily referenced pamphlet for public consumption authored by national reading researchers states:

> Many educators and parents are gravely concerned about the federal government's *Reading First* initiative. . . . *Reading First* derives from an incomplete and flawed research base, the National Reading Panel Report, and from government documents and regulations that substantially misrepresent the Report's findings. As a result, schools are now redefining their approaches to teaching and learning on the basis of inadequate research and overblown claims that promise quick fixes. In many places, teachers are being required to use scripted, one-size-fits-all commercial reading programs that are neither scientifically based nor suitable for all the children in their charge.[4]

The approved commercial programs were heavily based on isolated skill instruction and would have children in low-performing schools (those enrolling primarily low-income children of color) spend many hours on drills and worksheets, unconnected to meaningful text. Although no research supports instruction in phonics beyond first grade or instruction in phonemic awareness (the ability to distinguish and manipulate sounds in spoken words) beyond short-term exposure in conjunction with reading instruction, the approved programs demanded both.

Washington Post journalist Michael Grunwald, in an article titled "Billions for an Inside Game on Reading," is one of many who have written about the program and its ties to Republican cronyism:

> Five years later an accumulating mound of evidence from reports, interviews, and program documents suggests that *Reading First* has had little to do with science or rigor. Instead, the billions have gone to what is effectively a pilot project for untested programs with friends in high places. . . .
>
> The company that developed Voyager Passport [one of the "approved" *Reading First* commercial programs] was valued at $5 million in a newspaper article before *Reading First*. Founder Randy Best, whose Republican fund-raising made him a Bush Pioneer, eventually sold it for $380 million. He then put [Reid] Lyon [the Republican architect of *Reading First*] and [Rod] Paige [former George W. Bush secretary of education] on his payroll.[5]

Numerous other instances of cronyism have been identified with the program. In addition, the U.S. Department of Education's own Institute of Education Sciences issued an interim *Reading First* Impact Study that left program developers scrambling for excuses. This and subsequent reports indicated that while *Reading First* students may have improved scores on phonics, there was no improvement in comprehension (and isn't that the point?). As a result of these findings and the allegations of impropriety, it appears that, even though many school systems have been coerced into adopting *Reading First*, federal money was not approved to continue the program. A cautionary tale for decontextualized isolated skills and for greedy national policy makers intent on assisting political friends in "skilled" profiteering!

Skills in Meaningful Context

So what am I suggesting the appropriate teaching of "basic skills" in literacy should look like? While I have advocated, and still advocate, for the explicit teaching of vocabulary, strategies, and conventions, judging from responses to my previous writings, some have misunderstood my intentions. When I wrote about skills in *Other People's Children*, I wrote in the context of national curricular trends that virtually banned the teaching of skills, suggesting that they could be incidentally learned in what was referred to as "whole language" pedagogy. Many teachers received so little training in whole-language methodologies, however, that not only could they not figure out how to embed skills but they were also clueless about the entire process. For example, my own daughter's first-grade teacher described whole-language instruction as "the whole class reading the basal reader at the same time"!

The trend now, as I have discussed, is to relegate low-income children to senseless instruction divorced from any real literacy activities. Once again, in what the whole-language movement was originally initiated to counter, children are not reading, but doing worksheets and drills on "phonemic awareness." I believe that we have to find and hold fast to a middle ground. Children need to participate in real literacy activities, but some who do not come from homes that reflect school culture, need to learn the skills necessary for literate communication. To be clear, I believe that the ideal teaching of "skills" should be intentional and explicit, as well as be: (1) situated within engaging activities; (2) embedded in real writing, reading, and communication or, if taught in isolation, put immediately into the context of real writing, reading, and communication; and (3) taught flexibly when needed, rather than as an unvarying curriculum.

To clarify what this might look like in practice, let me provide a few examples from early literacy instruction, vocabulary development, and writing.

New Zealand's Don Holdaway, introducer of the "big book" (children's books printed in a size large enough for an entire class to read together) was cited early on by whole-language advocates in this country. Holdaway's focus on teaching phonics, however, was often ignored in the later iterations of the whole-language approach that often seemed to vilify all instruction that focused on directly teaching sound/symbol relationships. When the pendulum swung in recent years to teaching phonics and phonemic awareness through worksheets and exercises removed from books and stories, his work was still ignored. I believe that Holdaway's instructional models, however, provide a commonsensical alternative to both extremes.

In his seminal *Foundations of Literacy*, Holdaway presented detailed instructions to teachers on how to teach initial consonant sounds by using the text in real books and on what to do if children were not making use of phonological knowledge in their reading. Holdaway began with sharing stories in books, exciting children about literacy, and making connections between their lives and text. In the context of using "big books" and stories put on overhead projectors, he used various screening devices to cover some letters of words and thus focus children's attention to specific letters and letter combinations. He used poetry to get children to attend to the sounds of language and to help them see the consistency of the sound of some groups of letters. In one instance, he used a poem titled "K-K-K-Katy" to begin playing an initial consonant game which he and the children expanded to other words, such as "t-t-t-teacher" and "M-M-M-Monday," and so forth.

Holdaway's methods put the teacher squarely at the center of instructing children, rather than a scripted program that cannot adjust to students' needs. I quote extensively from his work because it is now so seldom available to teachers. Here he describes the activity of his kindergarten class:

A few children have caught onto the idea of letter-sound relationships after three or four explanations, but the majority haven't seen it. We decide to take the matter very carefully and introduce two highly contrastive letter-sound associations: "m" because the children can hum—and we have an extroverted Molly in the class— and "f" because it has a primal slippery sound and feel. Then we go looking in the familiar books we know, and we keep our eye out for "m" and "f" in the new stories.

Some of the little rascals scan the text way ahead of where we are up to and shout at inappropriate times, "There's an EM!" We learn how valuable it is to know how to start saying a word that we're expecting. We get into that delightful *Fun on Wheels* by Joanna Cole and find quick confirmation in "four" and "five wheels" for our beginning "f". Then comes "f_____ on wheels" with a picture of a parading carnival animal on wheels—"Wow! FLOATS on wheels!" and then, later, "Zip, Trip, F_____, on wheels" and sixty percent of them are there. Careful pairing of letter-sound relationships through "b," "g," "s," and "t"—all contrastive—brings insight for many of the children. The rest of the initial consonants and consonant blends are learned rapidly by those children in the following few weeks without specific instruction. For the remainder, a continuing programme of contrast and use brings insight at varying rates.[6]

Holdaway is constantly in tune with the needs of his students and uses the instruction of skills as a *means* to the real goal of reading, rather than as a goal in and of itself. When there is a need to continue explicitly teaching sound/letter correspondence he does so. When the need ceases to exist, he ceases the explicit instruction. The children are always actively engaged and excited about learning. There is a strong connection between the teacher and the students, the students and each other, and the students and text.

Another example of the kinds of skills instruction I advocate is embodied in the work of Stephanie Terry. Stephanie is a gifted teacher in Baltimore with whom I have been honored to work. Stephanie, now retired, taught first grade to low-income African American students for more than thirty years. Her students always learned to read and write by the end of their year with her. They always scored the highest in the school on any standardized tests.

I interviewed Stephanie quite a few years ago about her work. Stephanie believed in teaching "skills," but she also believed in introducing her students to children's literature from day one. She engaged her kids in engrossing and far-reaching discussions about books and worked at making connections between their experiences and those in books. She kept a variety of animals in her classroom that the students carefully studied and whose behavior they carefully analyzed. And her students "wrote," whether conventionally or with scraps of letters and pictures, from day one. They wrote about themselves, they wrote about the animals, they wrote about conducting science experiments, they wrote creative stories.

Stephanie also began phonics instruction after the first week. When I told her that this seemed inconsistent with the ideas of advocates of the current whole-language curriculum that had been adopted by her district, Stephanie countered with the statement, "I teach children, not curricula." In pressing her on the issue, I learned that she believed that it was important for children to learn what literacy was all about, to understand the purposes of texts, and to love words as she did, but that they also needed some explicit instruction about how the written code of language worked. She believed that other children got such knowledge at home but that her students were completely dependent on her to provide them with the knowledge necessary to become proficient readers and writers. She also believed that the children she taught might not have available to them someone to ask if they couldn't figure out a word, so they had to have tools to allow them to do it independently. That's where she saw phonics coming in. But, she stressed, you can't do phonics before children love literature and want to read and write, or it won't make sense. You just create people who don't see any point to it all.

One of the many engaging, explicit strategies Stephanie used to teach writing was a "big journal." All of the children wrote in their own journals daily. Stephanie created an oversized journal large enough for all the children to see at one time. She used the journal daily to write an entry as the children watched. She asked for their advice about identifying spelling errors (she deliberately misspelled words that the children typically misspelled in their own journals). She modeled using the class "word wall" when she couldn't think of or spell a specific word. She showed them how to use the editing "carrot" (caret: ^) to add missing words. She even helped them focus on issues of style by having the children decide whether she was being sufficiently descriptive, whether there was a better word to use to get her meaning across, or whether she gave enough information to make the story interesting to read.

By modeling the writing process, Stephanie taught the skills that children then used in their own writing. Watching the class engaged in the activity, I was always impressed with the children's focus and concentration as they helped "Ms. Terry" edit her writing. This instructional strategy is in stark relief to what I usually see in schools where children are given writing assignments that are sometimes "corrected," but the corrections are never reviewed by the teacher or given any attention by the students. The students are never given any actual instruction on how to write, and so they practice and become expert at the poor writing strategies they brought with them into the classroom!

Vocabulary development is one of the most powerful paths to literacy, especially for children who do not have access to the middle-class vocabulary that schools expect. Unfortunately, it is also one of the most poorly taught aspects of the curriculum. What is most evident in classrooms, particularly in classrooms that serve low-income children of color, are the strategies that have proven over and over *not* to work: looking up words in the dictionary; writing sentences with new words prior to any discussion and study of the words; being told to figure out the words in context (W.E. Nagy found that students reading *at grade level* had about a *one in twenty* chance of learning the meaning of a word from context[7]); and memorizing definitions. What does work is:

1. *Integration*: connecting new vocabulary to prior knowledge.
2. *Repetition*: encountering/using the word/concept many times.
3. *Meaningful use*: multiple opportunities to use new words in reading, writing, and discussion.[8]

All of the research informs us that we should teach vocabulary in meaningful contexts. According to researchers W.E. Nagy and P.A. Herman, middle-class children learn about three thousand words a year incidentally and only about three hundred from organized instruction. Nagy and Herman state further that because the bulk of children's vocabulary growth occurs incidentally, "the single most important goal of vocabulary development should be to increase the amount of incidental word learning."[9]

In my work in dozens of successful classrooms, effective teachers of low-income students of color take every opportunity to introduce students to complex vocabulary while also teaching needed conventions and strategies. Students are involved in activities that use the information and vocabulary in both creative and analytical ways. They play word games, exploring prefix and suffix meanings. They create metaphors and art work that connect new words or concepts to knowledge from their own experiences. They also explore new words and concepts as they memorize and dramatize texts that involve advanced vocabulary and linguistic forms. Dramatizations are performed for other students, parents, and the community at large.

Teachers engage students in exciting thematic units that are ongoing (like that of the teacher described above who created the Silk Road unit), reviewing important domain knowledge, and developing vocabulary through repeated oral and written use. Students are then asked to explain what they have learned to others, thus gaining more experience in working with new vocabulary and solidifying new knowledge.

Not only do the teachers and schools who are successful with low-income children practice these strategies, but other researchers[10] have documented the efficacy of the strategies as well. Successful instruction is constant, rigorous, integrated across disciplines, connected to students' lived cultures, connected to their intellectual legacies, engaging, and designed for problem solving that is useful beyond the classroom.

In short, what those who have been successful teaching low-income students to achieve at high levels know is that they do not need to "fix" the language of the parents or to devise some preschool intervention that will "fix" the children, or to "dumb down" instruction with scripted teaching. Rather, students need focused instructional strategies throughout their school years that are designed specifically for their cultural and academic backgrounds.

This is how the "basic skills" of the middle class should be acquired by children who do not possess them upon entering school. This is how middle-class parents, often without realizing it, teach their children. They build upon the children's interests; they ensure that the children are exposed to new settings; they discuss what the children have experienced while using new vocabulary. That is what we as teachers must do for our charges who do not bring to school the academic trappings of middle-class homes. And we must not only identify what they *don't* know but acknowledge and celebrate what they *do* know and bring with them to class—a maturity in problem solving, an ability to do what is needed in difficult situations, an understanding of real-world problems—that middle-class children are not likely to exhibit for years to come. They bring what schools sometimes disparage as "street sense," knowledge that is not only "higher order thinking," but that can be built upon to spur the acquisition of the "basic skills" that schools demand.

4

WARM DEMANDERS:
THE IMPORTANCE OF TEACHERS
IN THE LIVES OF CHILDREN OF POVERTY

*"My teacher treated me as a diamond in the rough, someone
who mostly needed smoothing."*
—Mary Frances Berry, *USA Today*

*"There comes that mysterious meeting in life when someone
acknowledges who we are and what we can be, igniting the
circuits of our highest potential."*
—Rusty Berkus, *To Heal Again*

I've taught many young teachers, and they all seem so tired when
they arrive at my evening classes. I know they work hard, and I
know that for many of them "the system," "the parents," "the pa-
perwork," "the high-stakes tests" all make it seem that what they
do doesn't make much of a difference. If there is one message I try
to convey to them, it is that *nothing* makes more of a difference in

a child's school experience than a teacher. As I have written before, when I interviewed a group of African American men who were successful but "should not" have been, based on their socioeconomic status, their communities, their parents' level of education, and so on, all of them insisted that their success was due in large part to the influence or intervention of one or more teachers during their school careers. These were teachers who *pushed* them, who *demanded* that they perform, even when they themselves thought that they could not. The teachers gave them additional help and insisted that they were capable of doing whatever anyone else could do.

Gloria Ladson-Billings says that successful teachers of low-income, culturally diverse children know that their students are "school dependent."[1] What she means is that while children from more privileged backgrounds can manage to perform well in school and on high-stakes tests in spite of poor teachers, children who are not a part of the mainstream are dependent upon schools to teach them whatever they need to know to be successful.

I am reminded of my own experience with my daughter in softball. To say that I am unknowledgeable about sports is an extreme understatement. Yet I wanted to make sure that my daughter was not handicapped by my limitations, so I took her to become a member of a locally sponsored team. Since my own knowledge of the sport did not extend beyond the names of the bat and ball, I was amazed that after two practices my seven-year-old actually knew where left field was! After practice, the coach came to talk to the parents. He told us that we needed to "work with" our kids at home, practicing softball skills and going over the rules. My first thought was panic, my second was, "Look, I get her here; you're the coach. It's your job to teach her. I can't do a thing." Suddenly I understood fully what many parents who are not school-savvy or educated themselves must think about schools and teachers who insist that they "work with" their children at home! If the coach didn't teach Maya, there was little hope for my child's future softball career.

For children of poverty, good teachers and powerful instruction are imperative. While it is certainly true that inequity, family issues, poverty, crime, and so forth all affect poor children's learning opportunities, British educator Peter Mortimore found that the quality of teaching has *six to ten times* as much impact on achievement as all other factors combined.[2] This can explain why I have found, like educator Robert Marzano, that two schools serving the same population can have vastly different success rates.[3] In a recent study of schools in a southern city, I visited two public elementary schools located less than a mile apart, both serving very low-income African American children. One school's state test scores were at the top of the district—higher than the average score of the district's well-to-do schools, and the other school's scores were at the very bottom of the district. What was the cause of such a discrepancy? The schools essentially served the same population. The difference could only be the quality of teaching and instruction. In each of the classrooms in the higher-scoring school I saw teachers engaged with their students, actually teaching. In the lower-performing school, I saw most teachers sitting while students completed seat work.

What gave me even more reason to pause was the realization that the teachers in the lower-performing school apparently believed that it was okay to remain seated and not involved with the students when a visitor came into the room. This was even the case when she or he observed my conversations with the students that made it clear that many of them did not understand what they were supposed to be doing on the worksheet. That observation led me to conclude that somehow the culture of the school signaled to the teacher that "not teaching" was okay. If there is not a strong culture of achievement in a school, many teachers may not be teaching as effectively as they are capable of doing.

Indeed, Mike Schmoker in his remarkable book *Results Now* cites a 2001 study by K. Haycock and S. Huang that shows that "the best teachers in a school have *six times as much impact* as the bottom third of teachers.[4] Much of Schmoker's work centers on the notion that poor children are not learning because schools and teachers are not adequately teaching them. He records instances of researchers and administrators visiting large numbers of classrooms and observing very little effective teaching and, despite district- or state-mandated curricula, very little coordinated, integrated instruction.

In my own recent visits to a number of schools and classrooms during a six-month stay in one mid-sized, predominantly African American district where I observed the two schools mentioned above, I was shocked to find how little teaching was actually occurring in many classrooms in a variety of schools. I saw an inordinate number of classrooms where students were doing seat work for an entire period—mostly busywork that had little connection to deep learning. Few if any questions were asked, and those that were demanded little thought on the part of student or teacher. Children who chose not to do the worksheet were ignored as long as they were quiet.

In one classroom of over-age high schoolers who had recently switched to a new schedule, the teacher told me that the periods were too long and the students got tired so she allowed them to take naps if they chose to take a break from doing their assigned seat work. In this language arts classroom, the teacher was apparently unaware that two students, instead of using the computers to complete their assignment, were instead comparing cell phone plans!

It is no surprise, but still a jolt, to realize the implications of such non-teaching. Schools that had been designated as "failing" had large numbers of teachers like those described. In contrast, schools that performed at high levels had larger numbers of teachers who were actually teaching. They were visible in the classroom. They held students' attention. They were explaining concepts and using metaphors to connect the knowledge students brought to school with the new content being introduced. They used different kinds of media. They asked students to explain concepts to their peers. They posed questions that required thought and analysis and demanded responses. *No one* was allowed to disengage.

One of the most poignant aspects of this reality is that students are quite aware when the instruction they are receiving is subpar. While many are willing to play the game to avoid being challenged, others are distraught at the realization that they are being shortchanged. In a Florida high school that has been designated as "failing" for several years in a row, the students were primarily low-income Haitian immigrants, many of whom were from Haitian Creole-speaking families. Many of those teaching in this school were substitutes or Spanish-speaking new immigrants with limited English skills themselves who were recruited from Central American countries because they knew a specific subject area but who had no teaching experience. A district math supervisor told me that she once visited the school and had to hold back tears when the students in one class looked at her pleadingly and said, "Miss, can you please teach us something?"

During my sojourn visiting schools, I also had the opportunity to talk with high school students who were involved in a citywide after-school spoken-word poetry-writing program. As I always do when I have the opportunity, I asked the primarily African American students to talk to me about what problems they saw in their schools. Most of the students' comments focused on what teachers did or did not do in classrooms.

Students were also very aware of the culture of their schools, the attitudes their teachers have toward teaching, and the effort those teachers put into their craft:

- It's bad when they say you go to a bad school. It's like then they think you are automatically a bad person. Even when it's just one bad seed that acts crazy, people think everyone in the school is like that.
- Sometimes the teachers won't give you help. Some of them say things like, "I got mine; all I have to do is get my paycheck."
- In high school a lot of teachers are about occupying us, not teaching us.
- The bookwork and the tests have nothing to do with us.
- Our teachers don't understand how much impact they have. It's hard when they act about as serious about what they're doing as our little sisters or brothers.
- One teacher said she didn't want to teach today because she was having a bad day. But then she would have about four or five bad days in a row!

I also asked them to describe a good teacher they had encountered in their school lives:

- A good teacher takes time, makes sure you understand.
- One who enjoys being there.
- One who doesn't put on a movie when they're tired.
- A teacher who asks questions to help get the students closer to the answers.
- For each chapter there should be a lecture, activities and games, and reading outside of the text from different sources (from a future teacher, perhaps?).
- One who has a sense of humor, but can be serious when necessary.
- Someone you can find outside of class for help.
- Someone who is patient, understanding, ready to teach if you're ready to learn.

- One who is willing to learn about you and about new things.
- A good teacher inspires you and pushes you to the point of no return.

Many researchers have identified successful teachers of African American students as "warm demanders." James Vasquez used the term to identify teachers whom students of color said did not lower their standards and were willing to help them. Warm demanders expect a great deal of their students, convince them of their own brilliance, and help them to reach their potential in a disciplined and structured environment.[5]

Franita Ware in her research describes several such teachers, including Ms. Willis, a sixteen-year veteran, who taught third through fifth grades. In one example of Ms. Willis's no-nonsense approach, she spoke loudly and clearly to her students about the importance of completing and submitting homework:

Chris, pass out the workbooks while I'm doing some housekeeping and I want everybody to . . . listen. Yesterday I checked for two things; number one, homework. I had about half of the class that turned in their homework. I do not give you homework every day, but when I do it's a practice skill that needs to be done. It's something that you need: it's not just something for you to do. . . . And I expect you to do it. Now from now on, if you cannot do it, then you need to write me a note of explanation. And the only reason I'll tell you that you cannot do your homework is that you are dead—and you won't be here then. Because if you go to Grady [a local hospital with a reputation for long waits], I told you all the time . . . take your book with you and do it while you're sitting there. . . . We are not here to play, I'm getting you ready for middle school. . . . I am thoroughly disappointed with you. . . . Excuse me for hollering.[6]

Ware comments that what was remarkable when observing this classroom is that the students were *"absolutely quiet and looked at her with respect* while she spoke."[7] They did not indicate any anger or resentment, but rather their facial gestures suggested remorse. Ms. Willis was explicit about why these students in a remedial class needed to do homework; at the same time she acknowledged that students were not always in control of their lives (e.g., perhaps having to spend the evening in the hospital). However, she gave students ideas for ways to resolve issues that might arise and take control of unforeseeable eventualities. There were no excuses.

Ms. Willis would tell her students who could not read that they *would* read and that she would teach them. Poverty is not seen as an excuse for failure with warm demanders. Although they recognize the difficult circumstances of their students, they demand that they can and will rise above them.

Another teacher studied by Ware, Mrs. Carter, expressed similar beliefs. She refused to accept poverty as an excuse for lack of academic achievement. When a student didn't own a computer, she still had to finish a computer-based assignment. Mrs. Carter allowed the student to come early and/or stay after school, and she wrote a pass for her to use the computer during the homeroom period. The point is, there are no excuses.

I know of another warm demander with an excellent reputation for producing high achievement levels with her low-income students. This elementary teacher sympathized with her young charge who would fall asleep every day in reading class. Although she knew that the child's home life was in shambles, she told the child that, no matter what, she had to work to learn in school. In order to keep the child awake and alert, the teacher had her stand during reading instruction. There was no ridicule involved, only support and praise for her efforts. If the child wished to sleep at recess, she could.

Teachers who are warm demanders help students realize that

they can achieve beyond anything they may have believed. One of my favorite stories about a warm demander comes from well-known motivational speaker Les Brown. After being abandoned as an infant by his young, single mother, who gave birth to him on a filthy floor in an unused warehouse in Liberty City, Miami, Brown and his twin brother were adopted by a single cafeteria worker. Because of his high energy and inability to focus, he was placed in an educable mentally retarded class in fifth grade. He says that because he was called slow, he lived up to the label. He languished in these classes until a chance encounter in his junior year in high school changed his life.

As he was waiting outside a classroom for a friend, the substitute teacher inside the class called out to him,

"Young man, go to the board and work this problem out for me."

"Well, I can't do that sir."

"Why?"

"I'm not one of your students, first of all."

"Go to the board and work it out anyhow."

"Well, I can't do that, sir."

"Look at me. Why not?"

"Sir, because I'm educable mentally retarded. I'm not supposed to be in here."

Brown says that as the students in the class erupted in laughter, the teacher, Mr. Leroy Washington, said, "Don't ever say that again. Someone's opinion of you does not have to become your reality."[8]

That comment was the turning point of Brown's life. Mr. Washington became his mentor. Brown followed Washington around, watched him, modeled his behavior, and wanted to be a great speaker like him. Brown believes that it was because of Mr. Washington's comment and his continued insistence that Brown would be what he believed he could be, that Brown became the remarkable success that he is today.

Brown spoke about Mr. Washington in an interview: "In his presence he made you feel, without uttering a word, that you had greatness within you. That man triggered something in me that reminds me of what Goethe said, 'Look at a man the way that he is and he only becomes worse, but look at him as if he were what he could be, then he becomes what he should be.'"[9]

Warm demanders are sometimes spoken of by their students as being "mean." For those teachers who master this pedagogy, their "meanness" is often spoken of with pride by their students, and often with a smile, "She so mean, she *makes* me learn."[10]

Tyrone Howard studied a teacher, Ms. Russell, who, although stern and self-identified as authoritarian, would always treat her students with respect. She referred to them as "Ms." or "Mr." and always explained why she chose to take various actions. Her students sometimes expressed discontent with her domineering ways of teaching, but most thought that the ends justified the means: "She's mean and she hollers a lot, but you learn. I know that I have learned a lot this year, especially in reading and math. And if you look at all of the kids who make the honor roll or honor society, they're mostly in her class, so I guess it's worth it."[11]

I have written elsewhere that we cannot assume that a raised voice carries the same meaning in all cultures. My great niece DeMya at five years old turned to me one day and said out of the blue, "When people's mamas yell at them, it just means they love them." Tyrone Howard found similar beliefs when he sought to get young students' responses to their teachers.

Jaylah, a fourth-grade student stated, "If you [a teacher] holler, it just means you care. But you can't holler for no reason at all. If we did something bad and she didn't holler, I would think that something's wrong, and maybe she [doesn't] care [any] more."[12]

My own caveat about interpreting the raised voices with which some teachers, usually African American, talk to children, is that it is important to listen to their words, not just their tone. Good teachers may be telling the children that they are "too smart" to be acting the way they are acting, or submitting the kind of work they are turning in (or not turning in). When a teacher expresses genuine emotion and a belief in a child's ability to do better, that is a message that many children are eager to hear, regardless of the medium.

Howard wrote of one teacher who became upset with one of her fourth-grade students because of the student's failure to complete a task. The teacher angrily told the student she was capable of better work. The student stood humbly without response. To an outsider this might have seemed harsh, but shortly after the teacher expressed her disappointment, she approached the girl, put her arm around her shoulders, and had a private conversation. The next day the teacher showed Howard a note she found on her desk in which the chastised student thanked the teacher for being so terrific and thanked her for her "toughness," because it "really got me back on track."[13]

I need to pause for an aside here, however. I want to make it clear that I am not suggesting that everyone should proceed to be mean to or yell at black children. That model typically works only when, as Mrs. Carter in Ladson-Billings's work suggests, your own cultural background is so similar that you also associate a raised voice with concern and caring. And there are certainly times when "yelling" by a teacher of whatever color is intended to belittle and degrade students. What I am saying is that real concern about students' not living up to their academic potential should be transmitted in the teacher's genuine mode of emotional expression. For many teachers, that mode could more likely be quietly expressed as disappointment. It could be expressed through humor. The point is to make sure the students know that the teacher believes they are capable and expects a lot of them.

It may be surprising to some that the students respond to such high expectations and strong demands. It is important to point out, however, that high expectations and strong demands are insufficient. The other necessary components are care and concern. When students believe that the teacher cares for them and is concerned about them, they will frequently rise to the expectations set. When students believe that teachers believe in their ability, when they see teachers willing to go the extra mile to meet their academic deficiencies, they are much more likely to try.

Recent empirical research has also supported the educational value of the "warm demander" model. In a study in Chicago that sought to determine what differentiated schools that improved from those that did not, Valerie Lee and colleagues found that schools that were the most successful maintained two elements. The first she calls "academic press," meaning that the content that students are to learn is made clear, expectations for academic learning are high, and students are held accountable for their performance and provided the assistance needed to achieve. This is the "demand" aspect of warm demanders. The second is termed "social support," meaning there are strong social relationships among students and adults in and out of school, the "warm" part of the warm demander equation. These relationships are imbued with a sense of trust, confidence, and psychological safety that allows students to take risks, admit errors, ask for help, and experience failure along the way to higher levels of learning. The greatest achievement occurred when both factors were present. When both existed, students made four times the yearly growth in math and three times the yearly growth in reading than when neither was present. If one existed without the other, the gains were much less impressive.[14] In schools with high academic press and low social support, the resulting performance of students was almost as low as if neither academic press nor social support was present. In other words, having high academic standards without providing the necessary social support essentially wiped out all potential gain. On the other hand, social support without academic press

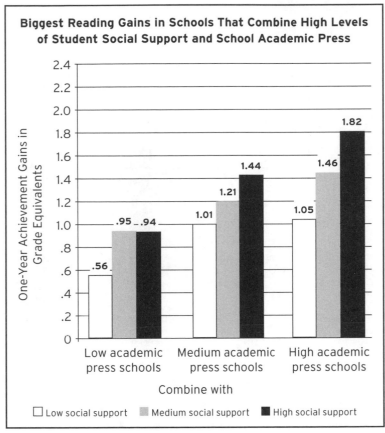

Figure 4. Valerie E. Lee, Julia B. Smith, Tamara E. Perry, Mark A. Smylie, *Social Support, Academic Press, and Student Achievement: A View from the Middle Grades in Chicago* (Chicago: Consortium on Chicago School Research, October 1999).

resulted in minimally higher performance than the inverse but still did not provide adequate academic growth.

Seminal scholar in multicultural education Geneva Gay has this to say about caring in the service of academic achievement:

Teachers have to care so much about ethnically diverse students and their achievement that they accept nothing less than high-

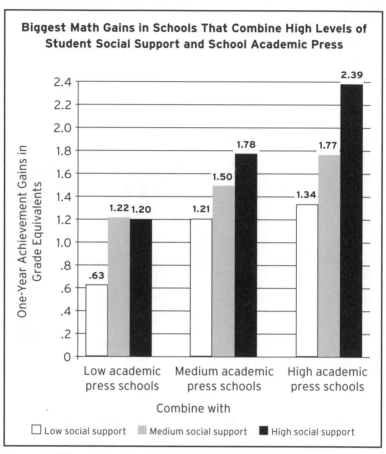

Figure 5. Valerie E. Lee, Julia B. Smith, Tamara E. Perry, Mark A. Smylie, *Social Support, Academic Press, and Student Achievement: A View from the Middle Grades in Chicago* (Chicago: Consortium on Chicago School Research, October 1999).

level success from them and work diligently to accomplish it. . . . This is a very different conception of caring than the often-cited notion of "gentle nurturing and altruistic concern" which can lead to benign neglect under the guise of letting students of color make their own way and move at their own pace.[15]

A part of this caring goes beyond academics. Warm demanders who are successful with children from poor families play other roles as well. They see themselves as advocates for the young people within a system that may not be so caring. They adopt many of the attributes of parents. They consider the whole child, not just his or her mind. They are concerned with the kind of people they are helping to mold—they focus on promoting character, honesty, responsibility, respect, creativity, and kindness.

I have seen miracles performed by many warm demanders over the years. Mr. Orlando Moss, a music teacher in Atlanta, for example, has been consistently able to mold young people with little or no musical background into a prize-winning orchestra—The William Still Sinfonia Orchestra. He demands hours of concentrated practice, much beyond the endurance (and attention span) of most adults. He tells the children, "I know you are tired, but I know you can play that measure with better tone. We will stay here all night if we need to." And the youngsters willingly put in more effort—even after their parents are grumbling and falling asleep in the bleachers. Of course, Mr. Moss will come in early or stay even later to help a young person who needs special attention.

I first met Mr. Moss when I brought my eight-year-old daughter to his orchestra class. He quickly said hello to me but directed intense attention to Maya. As he shook her hand, he looked deeply into her eyes and said, "Hello, prodigy." And that is how he greeted all of his new students—all black and Hispanic, most from low-income families.

I have seen the same warm demander pedagogy in teachers of all ethnicities. One of my daughter's young white high school teachers, Melissa Maggio, "read" my daughter's attitude of academic indifference correctly when she sat down with Maya for a long talk. Ms. Maggio finally broke through Maya's shell of nonchalance when she said, "You just don't think you're very smart, do you?" Through sudden tears, my child admitted the truth of that revelation. From then on, Ms. Maggio proceeded to prove to this child that she was indeed intelligent by pushing her relentlessly to excel.

It is the quality of relationship that allows a teacher's push for excellence. As I have previously written, many of our children of color don't learn *from* a teacher, as much as *for* a teacher. They don't want to disappoint a teacher who they feel believes in them. They may, especially if they are older, resist the teacher's pushing initially, but they are disappointed if the teacher gives up, stops pushing. One veteran high school teacher observed:

> Teaching anywhere today is hard work. It's especially hard in the cities because there are so many forces out there fighting against you. Teachers take the kids' resistance as not wanting to learn. But as soon as the teachers stop pushing, the students say that teachers didn't care because they would have kept on pushing them. The kids see it as a contest. Every day when I went into the classroom, I knew I had to be up to the challenge. I never understood, but I never gave up because I'm not a quitter.[16]

The caring, the persistence, the pushing—all these create trust. It is the trust that students place in these strong teachers that allows them to believe in themselves. It is the teachers' strength and commitment that give students the security to risk taking the chance to learn. These teachers do not shy away from a student challenge, but deal with issues when they arise. They seldom send a disruptive student to the office. They maintain their own discipline. They engage in conversations with disrupters outside of class to build the relationships that are the basis of cooperation. And these students know that if the teacher is strong enough to control them, then the teacher is strong enough to protect them.

Ware interviewed Mrs. Carter before the start of the school year and asked her about her disciplinary procedures:

Sometimes I *mean-talk* them in varying degrees of severity. And sometimes when you do yell, it is not always right to yell. Sometimes you have to go back and say—"What was really going on with you when I yelled at you? I'm so sorry"—you know, but what was really happening? . . . Sometimes with these kids, you have to [address the behavior] right then and there. . . . They are accustomed to a certain response and if you don't give them that response they will read that as weakness. "She's weak; I can do this and she won't even say anything to me." But if you turn around and you get them right there, where it is, and it doesn't matter who's there or what's going on, you don't have that problem.[17]

Although I contend that teachers of all ethnicities are capable of successfully teaching African American children, most of the teachers I have described here are themselves African American. Their success is not because their skin color matches their students' but because they know the lives and *culture* of their students. Knowing students is a prerequisite for teaching them well. There are several ways to become knowledgeable about one's students— living in their community, spending a lot of time there, talking extensively with students and their parents. But one of the most effective and efficient means is learning from excellent teachers who already know the students and their culture. One young European American teacher I met at a conference told me that she and an African American teacher in her school began some tough discussions about race, culture, and teaching after an incident had left them both upset. Eventually, in order to attempt deeper understanding of the positions each adopted after the incident, they decided to spend time observing in each other's classrooms. The teacher who spoke to me at the conference said that those observations and discussions were so enlightening that they changed her teaching forever.

Similarly, African American Jennifer Obidah, then a young professor, and Karen Teel, a seasoned white high school teacher, found themselves arguing about issues of race and teaching when they tried to work together on a research project. Rather than move away from the conflict, they agreed to move deeper into exploring their differences. The result was a co-authored book titled *Because of the Kids*, which can serve as an example of what white teachers can learn from black educators.[18]

And so, to my students who are teachers, and to all teachers, I reiterate: Your work *does* matter more than you can imagine. Your students, particularly if they are low-income children of color, cannot succeed without you. You are their lifeline to a better future. If you put energy and expertise into your teaching, learn from those who know your students best, make strong demands, express care and concern, engage your students, and constantly ensure that your charges are capable of achieving, then you are creating for your students, as Professor Bill Trent once said about his own warm demander teachers, "a future we could not even imagine for ourselves."[19]

5

SKIN-DEEP LEARNING:
TEACHING THOSE WHO LEARN DIFFERENTLY

A few years ago I was asked to contribute to the book *Learning Disabilities and Life Stories*, edited by Pano Rodis, Andrew Garrod, and Mary Lynn Boscardin.[1] The most powerful aspects of this book were the memorable and often startling autobiographical essays contributed by young people who had struggled with living and learning with learning differences. Their stories were poignant and painful reminders of how intolerant our educational institutions are of difference and how fragile the belief in oneself as a learner can be.

As I read the essays, Gretchen O'Connor's story of her struggles with ADHD touched on such familiar territory that I decided to share it with my daughter. Eyes wide with wonder, eight-year-old Maya stared at me. "Gee, Mom," she whispered in an awed voice, "that sounds just like me!" She was right; it did sound just like her. Although she had not been formally diagnosed with any learning or attentional differences, I had long suspected that her mind works in unique ways.

I admit I have sometimes been frustrated with her disorganization, the *hours* it could take her to complete the simplest tasks, her handwriting difficulties, her apparent inability to keep track of any of her belongings or to finish the many projects she begins. However, I would trade none of those traits if it meant I would lose her poetry (one of her poems as a seven-year-old refers to daffodils as "those flowers that stick out their big noses to sniff for spring"), her ability to play anything by ear on the violin (or almost any other instrument she picks up), her letters to the fairies, the amazing costumes she has designed for the various characters she's created, her visionary artwork (when asked to draw a picture of her room, she represented what I saw fairly well, and then drew flocks of multicolored birds all over the floor), her kindness to younger children, her ability to entertain herself with even the simplest of artifacts—an odd-shaped stick, a flattened stone, or an old tarnished fork—or the vibrant energy that she would bring to every act of living.

Like most mothers, I have always known her to be special, but, like many other children whose minds work in nontraditional ways, schools have sometimes seen her only as a bunch of problems to be solved. After a happy kindergarten year, Maya was so excited about going into first grade that when she woke up on Sunday morning she wondered if there were any way I could make her sleep until Monday so she wouldn't have to wait another day! When Monday morning finally came, she sang and skipped and danced her way to school, so happy she was about to burst. By Friday, she was crying in the morning, saying she had a stomachache and didn't want to go to school anymore. Every day she brought home packs of worksheets, marked with big red letters, "INCOMPLETE." Wanting to give the teacher and the school time, I decided to wait and see if things would settle down. By the end of the next week, she was still crying, still bringing home uncompleted worksheets, and, by Wednesday, sobbing that she wasn't going to get a treat on Friday because she had too many checks by her name.

It was time to pay the school a visit. When I entered the cramped classroom (the school was overcrowded, so the school system rented several small rooms from a church next door), I almost started sobbing myself. Her classmates were seated in very closely placed desks facing the blackboard. Her desk was at the back of the room facing a window. What I saw in my brief visit was a disaster for any child with attentional issues. While the children were supposed to be working on a worksheet copying words from the board to complete sentences from a three-lined "story" they had earlier reviewed, the teacher first discussed the lunch procedure and then welcomed another adult who presented the class with a caterpillar in a jar. After pondering aloud about the differences in the developmental stages of moths and butterflies, the teacher told the children to continue working on their worksheets while she read to them about caterpillars from the encyclopedia. I quickly realized why I saw so many unfinished worksheets coming home. Trying to fight back my own tears, I asked the teacher if I might be able to talk to her after school.

While waiting for the end of school, I secured the curriculum guides for first grade from the office. From these, I learned that the district embraced a "whole-language, literature-based, integrated curriculum." When I was able to speak with the teacher, I asked first about the curriculum. She informed me that "whole language" meant that "the whole class reads from the basals at the same time" and that I had seen an example of integrating science and language arts when she read about butterflies as the children were completing an unrelated reading worksheet and that "literature-based" meant that when the children finished all their worksheets, they could go out into the hall and read a book. I was dumbfounded at her interpretations of the curricular guide and was hardly hearing her when she went on to complain specifically about Maya. "She daydreams all the time, she won't finish her work, she doesn't pay attention, and she talks to her neighbors." The teacher went on to say that her job was to train Maya to be a student.

I tried not to sound as upset as I felt when I told her that, if she wanted Maya to pay attention, she might want to reconsider having her facing a window. Since I knew all of the children from the previous year, I suggested a possible seating arrangement that could minimize inappropriate talking. I also tried to explain that Maya was a very competent reader and could read all of the worksheets without difficulty. Her challenge was that she could not easily copy from the board or write quickly, because her motor skills were slower. I wondered if she might be able to read more books and copy less, as her motor skills were still developing.

The teacher told me that no, she knew what she was doing, and that I needed to "trust" her. After all, she had been teaching for fifteen years, and she knew what was best. The next day, I spoke to the principal about my concerns. She told me that "the purpose of first grade was to learn to sit in a desk," that Mrs. Linder was one of the best teachers in the school, and that I should "just learn to trust her."

By October, with no hope of a different perspective in sight, Maya was still bringing home packs of uncompleted worksheets on a daily basis. I had tried "trusting" everyone else, thinking that maybe I couldn't trust myself. Was I too emotional? Was I too overprotective of my child? While all of that was undoubtedly true, were they right to try to make her conform unilaterally and I wrong to try to get *them* to change?

As the first six-week grading period neared, Maya had begun to say she was dumber than everyone else in the class because she couldn't finish her work. She had not gotten to read one book in school. She started sticking holes in her clothes with scissors. On the day before the parent-teacher conferences, I got a call from the teacher saying that Maya had cut up the teacher's basal sentence strips and was in big trouble. I could not have asked for a more symbolically appropriate representation of the problem!

I then knew that I had to act. Clearly the entire district's philosophy ran counter to anything I believed to be in my child's best interest. I used my connections to find someone in a neighboring school district who might be able to help me locate a more appropriate public school. Even though I had to pay for Maya to attend, I found a first-grade teacher who understood children's need for movement and appreciated divergent thinking. Indeed, at the end of the year, all children got awards; Maya's was "for the having of wonderful ideas." Once more, she flourished, and once more she looked forward to the following school year.

Unfortunately, second grade brought a teacher much like Mrs. Linder in philosophy, if much more effective in execution. Faced with sitting in a desk all day and listening to the teacher talk, Maya once more shut down. When I discovered that we might have to return to our home district the following year because of overcrowding, I agonized over what to do. Finally, after long discussions with friends who had older children and much heartache over "abandoning" public schools, I enrolled Maya that October in The Atlanta School, a very small private school with a diverse student body and teachers who truly integrated the curriculum, focused on children's strengths, and demanded hard work.

By the time Maya entered fourth grade, she was flourishing at The Atlanta School. She informed me she was writing the story of her life. One day she wrote, "If I could do one thing for the rest of my life, I would go to my school. I love school." Not that she didn't have challenges—her handwriting was still tortured, but she began learning to type; she worked hard, with her teacher's help, to learn to stay focused; with posted reminder lists, repetition, and contracts, she slowly learned to be more organized. And her teachers loved and celebrated her creativity, pushed her to write more poetry, let her interpret social studies through dance, and repeated math concepts as often as it took for her to "get it."

As Maya continued to blossom in a school that was meeting her needs, I often wondered, "what if." What if I had not had the background to know her first-grade teacher's understanding of the curriculum was flawed? What if I didn't know the "right people" to talk to in order to find an appropriate school? What if I didn't have the money or the resources to find the right private school?

What would have happened is exactly what happens to thousands upon thousands of poor children and children of color every year. Their schools, unable to accommodate any behavior or learning style outside a narrow range deemed acceptable, teach them a lifelong lesson: They learn that they are incompetent, inadequate, damaged. They are left with a sense of rage and brokenness. As Lynn Pelkey, one of the *Learning Disabilities* book's young essayists said, "I was taught to hate myself."[2]

One of the major factors that allowed Maya to flourish was that both The Atlanta School teachers and I concentrated on her gifts, on those things she did well. Many children identified as having learning disabilities do not get such treatment. As other of the essayists put it:

> Gretchen O'Connor: My teachers and parents overlooked all the areas in my life where I was succeeding and instead concentrated on my faults.
>
> Lynn Pelkey: Why must the learning disability categories be classified around negative attributes? Can we not focus on strengths and positive attributes?
>
> Velvet Cunningham: I was judged for what I could not do and not for what I could do.[3]

As the essays in the book show, these children become packages of pathologies to be "fixed"—at best tolerated, more often rejected.

They feel stupid and unacceptable to the school. The result is that, unless unusually supported outside of school, they reject the school environment. They sometimes use anger as a defense or go inside themselves as they try to disappear from the classroom setting or even turn to drugs or alcohol as they attempt to numb their pain.

As hard as things are for the mostly middle-class and mostly white children with learning disabilities chronicled in the book, poor African American and other children of color with learning problems are even more likely to face psychological trauma. First, the schools often do not fully understand their learning problems. When these children have trouble learning, it is too frequently assumed that it's only because they *are* less intelligent. When put into special education classrooms, they are frequently labeled not as having a learning difference but as educable mentally retarded, behavior disordered, or learning disabled slow learners.[4]

Children or young adults from middle-class families who are classified as learning disabled are often told that they are intelligent but that there's a part of their brain that works differently. If their parents locate supportive professionals, they are told that their children can learn just like everyone else but that they must find settings that meet their specific learning styles. By contrast, the explicit or implicit message to many poor African American children and their parents is that they are unable to learn, are intrinsically less intelligent, and must be isolated because they cannot be trusted to act like civilized human beings. The results are predictable.

After an article about my work appeared in a local paper, I received a letter from an African American man who was in prison for life. He was a very thoughtful man, who was concerned about the young men who were regularly imprisoned with him. He felt that these young men were full of rage, cared little about themselves or each other, and had very little academic knowledge. He had become a father figure to many of them. He wrote about what he perceived to be their major problem—the school systems that had shunted them aside and refused to educate them. He was especially concerned with the "special remedial" programs, which, for these young men, seemed to him to be a specialized track to prison. Almost every one of the young men he encountered in prison had been in "special" classes for much of his life. Given the overrepresentation of African American boys identified as behavior disordered or mentally retarded in special education classes, the impact on African American communities seems inevitable.

Yet many of the teachers in special education classes are committed educators. Why are the results so often problematic? One reason seems to be that once children are labeled with a "disability," then whatever learning issue they might have is reified into a permanent "condition" that becomes who they are rather than an indication of what assistance they might need. In the "high incidence" areas in African American populations (behavior disordered and learning disabled, for example), researchers Beth Harry and Janette Klingner found that those identifications were frequently not due to some internal condition of the child but to external conditions, many school influenced. For example, children who performed poorly had often received inferior prior instruction, or disruptive changes to a child's home life might cause temporary emotional trauma.[5]

Claude Steele's research on "stereotype threat," previously discussed in Chapter 1, in which individuals internalize the negative stereotypes held about them by the larger society, might help to explain not only why many African American students fare poorly in special remedial classrooms but also why those placed the earliest in special education classes seem to sustain the most damage from their school experiences. It is not necessarily the teachers nor the classes themselves that cause the problem but the early labeling as "less than."

Certainly, some students need specialized assistance. But why must a school brand them with labels that only cause their teachers, their peers, and ultimately themselves to focus on their weaknesses rather than on nurturing their strengths? At Renfroe Middle School in Decatur, Georgia, special education classes, known as "Critical Thinking" courses, were fully integrated into the general curriculum. They were scheduled during an elective block, and because of the name chosen to appear on the rosters, there were always requests from students at all performance levels to enroll.

Steele's research also found that identifiable remedial programs for socially stigmatized groups exacerbate the problem, causing students to perform even more poorly by possibly reinforcing the belief that they are less capable than others. He suggests instead that such students receive the necessary support to succeed in the context of a challenging curriculum that also provides instruction in areas in which they need extra help.[6] This idea is supported by Harry and Klingner, who question the notion of having to label children in order to provide them with assistance. Since we are all on a continuum of performance, how can we identify one specific point that determines a "disability?" Why not instead just provide children with the additional assistance they need and forgo applying a questionable label?[7]

Of course, there are many instances when lowered expectations coincide with a less challenging curriculum. I am haunted by one student's description of the "retard room."[8] It was bright and colorful—like a kindergarten—and without the accoutrements of an age-appropriate learning environment, such as maps. The unspoken message said loudly and clearly to this student that learning-disabled kids didn't need to learn "that kind of stuff." But even more troubling is this student's description of the teaching and learning within those classrooms:

The teachers were very kind, but I believe now that they under-estimated me. I would do what they told me to do, recite what they told me to recite, but I was rarely asked to really *think,* and I almost never experienced those moments when something I was learning came together and made sense.[9]

It is hard to comprehend why, in the name of "helping" children with special needs, we would confuse them with disconnected knowledge bites and make them feel stupid because nothing makes sense. It is even more difficult for me to fathom how this kind of teaching has become commonplace in "regular" education in many inner-city schools.

When I would visit The Atlanta School, a well-worn build-ing with children's artwork all over the walls and few resources (only one Internet-connected computer for the entire school, for example), the children would run up to me with great excitement. The littlest ones, the three- and four-year-olds, told me about their studies of the ear canal or showed me their portraits of Thelonius Monk and Miles Davis and asked me to listen to the blues songs they had created. The second and third graders rushed to tell me about what they had found out in their study of the history of medicine (the Babylonians used mallets instead of anesthesia!), ex-plained the ecosystem they were creating, showed me their draw-ings of constellations they'd studied and acted out the myths from the different cultures they each represented, or described the play, novel, or book series they were writing.

When I first enter some of the inner-city schools I work with—worn buildings with teacher-created bulletin boards all around and few resources—the children run up to me with equal excite-ment. When asked to share what they're learning, these children proudly present their neat handwriting or their latest worksheet. Although there is nothing intrinsically wrong with neat handwrit-ing and worksheets, there is a problem when these represent the limits of the teaching and learning taking place in a classroom—when isolated bits and pieces are presented to students without the "big stories" that make the pieces make sense. As surely as the children in "the retard room," these children are being robbed of a connected, comprehensible education.

Of course, neither all special education nor all inner-city classrooms are like that. Lita Sandford's special education classroom at Oakhurst Elementary in Decatur, Georgia, was frequently mistaken for the "gifted" class by short-term visitors, as children used computers to solve complex problems and created science reports with soundtracks and scanned-in photographs. And I am privileged to know many teachers in inner-city schools who create magical classrooms that surround children with excitement and learning. The problem is that these classrooms are still the exceptions.

There is one important lesson that The Atlanta School and other classrooms and schools that create meaningful, connected educational environments have taught me: What we call "the arts" provides a model to ensure that all children can learn without being labeled. Many accomplished African American adults can recall from their childhood the people who offered experiences that allowed them to be in touch with the magic they carried inside them, educators who "deliver the human being to himself," as actress Phylicia Rashad writes in a forthcoming book on arts and education.[10] When we see a child through the lens of the arts, we have the potential to see the child not only as he or she is but as he or she could be. Just as Rashad's teachers recognized something in her that they were led to "groom," we can see a child's strengths rather than his or her challenges.

Suddenly, the little boy who can't sit still, jumping and tumbling around the classroom, can, with a new set of lenses, become a potential dancer. The girl whose school papers are covered in scribbles becomes an artist. The boys who annoy their teachers by constantly tapping on their desks with pencils become drummers.

Those whose notebooks are filled with raps become lyricists, and that little girl who cries at the least affront becomes a thespian. The arts give us new eyes to see the potential for the expression of genius in our children. They also give us the opportunity to help children grow, rather than to constantly see their deficiencies. After all, isn't what we call the arts what our children do as their most natural expression, as they learn to live in this world? One need only spend a short time watching a toddler or a kindergartner interact with the world to see dance, the creation of sounds with voice or "instruments," visual expression through any available media—using all senses to explore and transform their environments. This is what children do.

But what do we ask of them when they come to school? Typically, we ask that they give up every natural instinct. Rather than help them discipline their natural instincts, we ask them to abandon every tool they have used to learn about the world and sit still and listen.

I had the amazing opportunity years ago to visit the Reggio Emilia Preschools of Italy, described by education pundits as the best preschools in the world. The schools use the arts to teach young children. I will never forget the sight of diapered babies—many of whom could not yet walk, sitting and crawling around outside on large pieces of newsprint, exploring, when they had a mind to, the pieces of charcoal wedges around them and making marks on the paper. There was a "teacher" sitting near every two or three babies, who would occasionally demonstrate a specific way to hold the charcoal, or a way to create shading, but the babies were free to imitate, explore, or ignore.

By the time these children were in the three-year-olds' room, the art they were creating was phenomenal. They had acquired the knowledge to use—with no admonitions to be careful—sharp pieces of glass in mosaics, pointy and sharp professional clay-working tools, and real china in the dress-up corner. By the time they were five years old, they were studying the science of the motion of the earth by exploring shadows and the physics of light and color spectrums in prisms and graphing mathematical proportion in to-scale drawings and clay-designed replicas of dinosaurs and skyscrapers. They wrote and performed plays stemming from their "play" in the dress-up corners. In short, these young children not only expressed themselves through the arts, they also learned what we consider to be mathematics, the sciences, and literate writing, and they learned without anyone labeling any of them because they chose to explore the world from a different pathway.

When Maya was nine years old, a psychologist at my university made some preliminary assessments of my daughter's learning. Her initial scores on several subtests were very low. Because the professor knew me and had come to know Maya, he decided to re-test her on that and several other subtests two days later. Upon retesting, her score on one subtest moved from the eighth percentile to the eighty-ninth percentile and jumped equally dramatically on the others. In schools, children who are poor and who belong to racial minorities are almost never retested. Even though the tester may have caught the child on a bad day or did not consider the differences between the child's culture and the assessment tool, the low score meets with the school's expectations of their group ability. We all mouth the mantra "All children can learn." I would modify the chant to "All children *do* learn." It's just that some of them learn that we expect them to be successful, and some learn from us that they are dumb. Whatever we believe, they learn.

The issue of how we teach children to think of themselves brings to mind an opportunity I once had to witness a group of dynamic African American high school students from my hometown of Baton Rouge, Louisiana, who were presenting at a national educational research conference in New York. The students, with the assistance of Petra Munro Hendry, a local university professor, had conducted the previously mentioned carefully researched oral history project about their high school, one of the first high schools created after the Civil War for black students in the South. Their research methodology and the data they had gathered were impressive and worthy of professional researchers. Their presentation, with the accompanying visuals and audio feed, was both engaging and thought provoking. As they concluded their findings, the audience gave them a standing ovation.

A question-and-answer period followed. An audience member asked about the current racial mix at the high school, whether there were now white students enrolled, and if so, if any of them had participated in the research project. One of the young people responded, "Oh, yes, there are white kids at our school, but we don't ever work with them because they're all gifted." There was a stunned silence until one of the group's sponsors explained that their high school, located in what was still the heart of the black community, was a magnet program for gifted students and that all of the white students in the school were in a separately run "gifted" program that shared no classes or resources with the all-black "regular" program.

As the implications of this revealing new information sank in, there was another hush in the room until an audience member rose to her feet and spoke with great power and authority: "Young people, do not ever say that the word "gifted" does not belong to you. You have proven through your work and your presentation that *you* are gifted. Someone else giving a label for political reasons has no relevance to you. *You* are gifted. Remember what you have done today and remember who you are and what you are. Thank you for your brilliance!" The room was electrified with applause and shouts of approval. One could only ponder the messages that the "regular" program youngsters who did not attend the conference received on a daily basis from the very existence of a program in their midst where only white kids could be "gifted."

The reality is that all children have much greater potential than we ever imagine, but our rigid educational system assumes that some children are incapable of achieving academically and that one model of instruction fits all. Schools that recognize differences without negatively stereotyping children, believe in all children's potential, and implement challenging instruction that embraces children in all their splendid variety can, as The Atlanta School did, teach to and develop children's strengths. Schooling that labels children as broken or tries to "fix" them to match the school's limited modes is doomed to failure.

Learning styles, like the language we speak and the skin we wear, are not separate entities to be "fixed" but part of the essential nature of any human being. If we can see all of the children we teach—skin color, culture, learning styles, income level notwithstanding—as complete, deserving, brilliant human beings, then perhaps we will manage to create the educational system we need. Education for *all* children should be "special"—that is, specially designed to discover the strengths and accommodate the needs of each child.

6
"I DON'T LIKE IT WHEN THEY DON'T SAY MY NAME RIGHT": WHY "REFORMING" CAN'T MEAN "WHITENING"

This story starts in 1954 with the *Brown v. Board of Education* decision and illustrates an interesting way in which education policy seems to repeat itself, often to the detriment of black children and the black community. Many educators today don't realize some of the "unofficial" repercussions of the desegregation decision. Prior to that ruling, black teachers and principals were guaranteed jobs in the segregated system. Whites taught white children in white schools and blacks taught black children in black schools. Often black teachers and principals were more highly degreed than their white counterparts, as work in black schools was one of the few avenues of employment open to highly educated African Americans.

When desegregation was forced into southern states, whites were determined to keep as many white teachers and white principals employed as possible. Hence, desegregation led to an initially unexpected opportunity for whites in education. In 1954, about 82,000 black teachers were responsible for teaching 2 million black children. In the eleven years immediately following *Brown*, more than 38,000 black teachers and administrators in seventeen southern and border states lost their jobs.[1]

In Arkansas, for instance, virtually no black teachers were hired in desegregated districts from 1958 to 1968. In Texas, five thousand "substandard" minimally or uncertified white teachers were employed to teach in formerly all-black schools, while certified black teachers were told to go into other lines of work.[2]

Black principals fared even worse. By some estimates, 90 percent lost their jobs in eleven southern states.[3] Many were fired, and others retired. Still others lost their jobs for minor transgressions, such as failing to hold monthly fire drills. Those who stayed were often demoted to assistant principal or to coaching or teaching jobs. Others were offered clerical or even janitorial work.

In 1964, Florida had black principals in all sixty-seven school districts. Ten years later, with integration under way and the black school-aged population growing, only forty districts had black principals. In North Carolina, the number of black principals dropped from 620 to 40 from 1967 to 1971. In 1954 Kentucky had 75 black principals. In 1968 there was 1.

Famed Louisiana educator J.K. Haynes, in a 1968 newspaper article titled "Veteran Educator Bemoans Loss of Negro Teachers and Principals," wrote, "It is a strange thing to me that in nearly every instance the assumption is that a black principal is inferior."[4]

A National Education Association task force sent to Mississippi to investigate issued a statement that said, "Black educators are being dismissed, demoted, and pressured into resigning from desegregating school systems: blacks are then replaced by whites without regard to qualification."[5] Northwestern University sociologist Johnny Butler, originally from Louisiana, published a paper in the 1970s in the *Journal of Negro Education* titled "Black Educators in Louisiana—a Question of Survival."[6]

Butler explains that while there were no laws in Louisiana to prevent black teachers from being displaced, there was a federal ruling that applied to the Deep South that should have protected their jobs. It stated that "if in any instance where one or more teachers or other professional staff members were to be displaced as a result of desegregation, no staff vacancy in the school system should be filled through recruitment from outside the system unless no such displaced staff member is qualified to fill the vacancy."[7] This meant that in order to give positions to new, white teachers, strategies had to be devised to remove black teachers from the system altogether.

Butler found that this was accomplished by claiming that the black teachers were incompetent, by closing black schools, and by demoting current black staff to lower positions. He quotes a few of the interviews he gathered with dismissed or demoted teachers:

> Friday, I was called into the office. The principal said, "Miss _____ I don't like what I have to tell you but I want you to resign." His reasons were 1) failure to develop certain reading skills, 2) allowing pupils to read a reader before they were ready to start with it—inability to handle the job. The principal made no earlier comments concerning his reasons for my dismissal. Had he done so, the errors which he said I made could have been corrected.
>
> *—MA certified, tenured, 6 years of experience*[8]

The teacher stressed that she was taken completely by surprise and had not been consulted about the reasons for her dismissal at an earlier date.

Another instance:

> The first time I became ill my principal carried me home and asked for my retirement without any full statement or anything. . . . I

can't see why he would ask for a retirement because of illness, or because someone is out for a few days. I was given the option, retire or receive a letter of dismissal.

—*MA certified, tenured, 12 years of experience*[9]

Logically, Butler claims, educators with MAs would have had greater immunity from displacement. But the opposite was true. The data collected for this study revealed that those with MAs had a higher percentage of displacement in all categories.

All of this created another issue. Many white students fled the district to private academies. And many white teachers did not want to teach in predominantly black schools. Thus, those white teachers reassigned to black schools (usually those with less experience and tenure) wanted to leave. State guidelines said that any teacher transferred had to remain in his or her post for three years. Most of these teachers then transferred out after the three years, creating an ever-changing array of young, white, inexperienced teachers in predominantly black schools.

A cartoon published near this time shows a long line of white teachers entering and exiting a revolving door, while a group of black children stare in bewilderment.

And now let us imagine that this same cartoon is published in the paper today. Could it possibly be applicable? In December 2008, *Time* magazine published a cover picture of Michelle Rhee, later the infamous superintendent of Washington, D.C., schools, holding a broom. The message: she is sweeping out "bad teachers."[10] The problem is, the teachers being swept out in D.C. and all over the country are veteran teachers, frequently black, who are working in low-income black schools.

And who are they being replaced with? Just as in the 1970s cartoon, a long line of minimally certified, undertrained, white teachers who will largely leave after two years of teaching service.

History has a way of repeating itself, and black children have a history of being the pawns in other people's agendas.

The emblematic—although certainly not the only—program for this effort is Teach for America (TFA). Founder Wendy Kopp crystallized her plan while she was a senior at Princeton and wrote a thesis on mandatory national service, focusing on a teacher corps for low-income areas. After college, she succeeded in securing corporate funding for her project, and by 2008, TFA's IRS 990 shows that the organization had revenues of $159 million. Recently, TFA received $50 million in federal taxpayer money from the U.S. Department of Education to continue its work.[11]

In two decades, Teach for America's approach to eliminating educational inequality has not changed: Recruit smart, hard-working graduates from Ivy League and other highly competitive universities and ask them, after a short training course, to take a hiatus from their future careers to commit two years to teaching in a low-income urban or rural school.

I have worked with a number of TFA teachers. Many, though not all, are tremendously dedicated, hard-working young people who want to do their best for the low-income black and brown students they teach. Often they are struggling and having great difficulty in the culturally foreign, educationally challenging setting in which they find themselves. Some, albeit not many (perhaps 20–35 percent, although the exact numbers are hard to discern), continue to teach beyond their two-year commitment. The longer they teach, of course, the better they become. But most do not stay long enough to become excellent in the job.

Many teachers and teacher unions, while annoyed by the halos that the media have placed around the heads of TFA teachers, did not pay TFA much attention initially. With the slowing economy, however, districts are laying off veteran teachers—many African American—and yet still hiring TFA recruits. In the summer of 2009, Boston Teachers Union president Richard Stutman met with eighteen local union presidents, "all of whom said they'd seen teachers laid off to make room for TFA members," according to an article in *USA Today*. Stutman added, "I don't think you'll find a city that isn't laying off people to accommodate Teach for America."[12]

In the Mecklenburg district of Charlotte, North Carolina, the superintendent laid off hundreds of veteran teachers but spared 100 TFA-ers. TFA expanded into Dallas in the fall of 2010, bringing in nearly 100 new teachers, even though the district laid off 350 veteran teachers in the 2008–2009 school year. In D.C., former TFA corps member and then superintendent Michelle Rhee laid off 229 veteran teachers in October 2009, but only 6 of the 170 TFA teachers in the system, according to the *Washington Post*.[13]

An Internet search provides numerous reports of veteran teachers being laid off and new recruits from TFA and similar programs being hired: In May 2011, while thousands of New York teachers faced the threat of layoffs, the city recruited 400 new teachers from New York City Teaching Fellows and 100 from Teach for America.[14] In April 2011, over 200 teachers without tenure were told by the Kansas City, Missouri, School District that their contracts would not be renewed. Many of the positions would likely be filled by the 150 recruits from Teach for America sought by Superintendent John Covington.[15] In the 2010–2011 school year, the Clark County School District of Las Vegas had to cut 540 teaching jobs to help close a $145 million budget deficit. Yet in addition to the 308 teachers Teach for America has supplied to Clark County over the past six years, the district expects to place 50 additional recruits in the 2011–2012 school year.[16] On the heels of laying off more than 900 teachers, the Houston Independent School District hired 213 corps members during the 2010–2011 school year, said Pamela Kaiser, Teach for America's public information coordinator. The contract for 2011 to 2012 anticipated hiring about 100 new Teach for America recruits.[17]

According to education journalist Barbara Miner, there is also growing tension between schools of education and TFA over jobs for new teachers. The College of Education at the University of Illinois at Chicago (UIC), for example, graduates about 300 certified teachers a year. The graduates, especially elementary teachers, are increasingly having difficulty finding jobs in Chicago schools. Victoria Chou, dean of the UIC College of Education, says, "One reason is the number of jobs committed to Teach for America and similar programs, which have arrangements with the Chicago public schools."[18] TFA has recently expanded into Alabama as well. According to a February 18, 2010, press release from Governor Bob Riley's office, 90 TFA teachers were to be incorporated into the "black belt" schools over the course of three years. At the same time, veteran teachers in Alabama are being dismissed. It is not too difficult to imagine which teachers are being replaced in the "black belt."[19]

In New Orleans, an announcement came out in May 2008 that indicated that TFA was planning to double the number of TFA teachers to 500 in the 2009–2010 school year. In 2010–2011 the numbers increased even further. Paul Vallas, then head of the

New Orleans Recovery School District, "surplussed" (read "dismissed") 150–200 veteran teachers to make room for more TFA and TeachNOLA (a similar local program) positions. Lance Hill, executive director of the Southern Institute for Education and Research in New Orleans (who occasionally refers to the program as "Bleach for America"), says, "This is the pattern: Vallas contracts with TFA and TeachNOLA for several hundred openings, then brings in 240 TFA teachers this summer and fires an equal number of veteran teachers, mostly black. This unprecedented practice of "set-asides" for mostly young, white, temporary teachers has had a disastrous effect on teachers who endured the worst conditions in the schools and are fighting to rebuild their lives after [Hurricane Katrina]. They get fired to make way for novice teachers who will leave the city and its problems when their two years are up."[20]

According to researcher Howard Nelson (in a personal communication), the teaching force in New Orleans was 73 percent African American prior to Hurricane Katrina, and is now only 56 percent African American. This is in a city where over 95 percent of the students are African American.

As alarming to me as the reductions in black teachers are the newer efforts to push TFA graduates into administrative positions in school districts. According to Heather Anichini, TFA managing director of teaching and school leadership, TFA aimed to have more than eight hundred alumni leading their own schools or school districts by 2010. To achieve that goal, TFA has partnered with a number of organizations and universities. New Leaders for New Schools offers TFA graduates clear, simplified pathways to becoming a school principal. "Building Excellent Schools," for example, provides paid internships for TFA alumni to become principals.

Although I haven't found exact numbers, because a minority of the TFA teachers are African American, the numbers of African Americans recruited to become principals cannot be very high. Regardless of ethnicity, however, these are young, minimally experienced individuals typically from distant cities. TFA boasts of its partnership with over 150 graduate schools offering TFA alumni benefits, such as two-year deferrals, fellowships, course credits, and waived application fees (what New Orleans writer and activist Kalamu Ya Salaam calls "welfare for the well-to-do")—with Harvard being the overall top choice of TFA alumni. All of this is designed to ensure that young people from faraway communities, with as little as two years teaching experience, are groomed to become principals in overwhelmingly black and brown schools.

What is all of this doing to our children and to our schools? A primary concern I have is that the message going out very strongly is that people who look like the African American children in the classrooms are not good enough to teach them. I am disturbed by this growing trend in urban systems, which seems to belittle the value of experienced African American teachers and imply that young, inexperienced, minimally trained European American college graduates are the salvation of low-income students of color. Post-Katrina New Orleans, cited as a harbinger for what is to come in urban districts around the country, is a case in point. Shortly after the Katrina disaster, the entire New Orleans teaching force—mostly African American—was fired. Although other districts around the country snapped up many of these teachers, New Orleans policy makers have been slow to rehire. Instead, they, along with private foundations, have sought to replace those experienced teachers with young, predominantly European American, alternatively certified, and Teach for America recruits. The Los Angeles–based Broad Foundation, the Seattle-based Gates Foundation, and the Fisher Fund of San Francisco joined together for the first time in order to provide $17.5 million to New Orleans, primarily to recruit and provide short-term training for "new" teachers and principals, most of whom will be neither from New Orleans nor share the culture of the predominantly African American student body.[21]

I do not wish to berate the young people who seek to teach through these programs. Many are idealistic and wish to make a difference in the world (although some I have interviewed talk more about building their résumés). Some will stay on to become excellent teachers; however, without the tutelage of experienced, culturally knowledgeable mentors, over 50 percent will be gone in two years, and over 80 percent will be gone after three years.[22]

We know that first-year teachers are least able to produce positive growth in their students and that teaching quality increases dramatically for the first three years before leveling off in the fourth year of teaching.[23] Thus, the constant replacement of second- and third-year teachers with new recruits will mean by definition that we will provide a substandard education for children in low-income urban schools, where such alternative teacher selection programs are situated.

I do not propose that we terminate these programs, but we must ask alternatively certified, young, idealistic teachers to make a longer commitment to education to ensure that our most fragile students are not subject to constant teacher turnover. Further, we must use some of the money we pour into alternative certification programs to provide long-term, careful training for a cadre of teachers who are committed to long-term service in low-income communities and who are extraordinarily skilled in all that we know about teaching children from culturally diverse communities. Otherwise, as one New Orleans community activist told me, we are providing low-income schools with tourists rather than teachers. We also know that, quality held constant, those who are most familiar with the students they are teaching are most likely to teach them well. If we are to successfully incorporate young, less-experienced recruits into the teaching force, we must ensure that quality, experienced educators who know and understand the students served by the school are there both to serve the students and to help mentor new, young, culturally unfamiliar teachers.

*   *   *

It's hard to overestimate how important it is to be known, especially in southern black communities. I've recently returned to my hometown in Louisiana after having lived away for many years. What strikes me more than anything is what I've started to refer to as "the dance of place," that I engage in several times a day:

> "Delpit? Did you go to St. Francis? Do you know any Guerins?"
> "Yes, I went to school with Tyrone."
> "Oh, he's my husband! We have to get together."

or

> "Did you live over by the Variste's on Lettsworth? You must have known my uncle. He was the minister over at Mount Olive."

or

> "Your mama taught my uncle, Glenn Darensbourg, over at McKinley."

or

> "I think you're my cousin!"

This is a means by which connections are made, a sense of belonging established, a feeling of order restored. When none of one's teachers can engage in that dance because they just arrived in the city, connections are harder to create, shared purpose more difficult to come by. When a child cannot connect the attitude and perspectives of a teacher with the attitudes and perspectives of community people who love him, understanding suffers. When teachers stumble over the unique names common to a place, then there is a deep disconnect. As one New Orleans child summed this up, "I don't like it when they don't say my name right."

I recently visited a charter school serving African American high school students in a large Midwestern district. All but one of the teachers were European American. Most were young and were seeking alternative certification. In what I thought was a courageous request, one of the administrators asked me to sit down with a group of ninth graders to find out what they really thought about the school. Several of the students immediately said they thought the teachers were too young, that it was hard to take them seriously, even if they yelled. I asked them who they would go to talk to at the school if they had a problem. Almost in unison they said the name of the office secretary (I'll call her Ms. Rigby). I asked why, and they responded that she was older, she was African American, and she could relate to what they were telling her. But, they added, Ms. Rigby didn't play, and if they were on the wrong track, she wouldn't hesitate to "bust" them, even if afterward she would give them a hug. "She's like your mama or your auntie," one of the students added.

I then asked if any of them had failed a class. "Roy," the epitome of cool, sprawled in his chair, head cocked, eyes hooded, waved his hand. This was his first entry into the conversations. I asked if he knew why he failed. "Yeah," he answered dismissively, "I didn't do the work." I asked why he hadn't done it. "Didn't want to." I then queried the group about whether they had ever had a teacher who made them *want* to work hard. Each one except Roy described a former teacher who was "nice," or whom they liked so much they "didn't want to disappoint," or who made them laugh and made learning fun. Trying to draw him in, I asked cool Roy what he would do if Ms. Rigby were his teacher. Suddenly, his whole demeanor changed. He sat up straight and said, "I'd do my work. I'd do my work all the time. You got to be scared of Ms. Rigby [said with a smile]. If she was the teacher it would be totally different. I have respect for her."

The young teachers in this school had a potential mentor in their midst that they weren't even aware of. They could learn a lot from Ms. Rigby. They could learn even more if they had teacher colleagues on the faculty with Ms. Rigby's background and cultural knowledge. In the same school where Ms. Rigby reigned, I asked another group of students to tell me about their teachers. They started telling me about Mr. Stieber and how great he was. I asked if Mr. Stieber was black or white. Well, they said, he's really black, but he looks white. One student said, to chuckles and general agreement, "He's white on the outside and black on the inside—he's a reverse oreo!" They continued with all kinds of accolades: "He's cool." "He's great." "He's real."

I later went to Mr. Stieber's class, expecting to see a young white man who had adopted black lingo, dress, and style. Much to my surprise, he was dressed in a suit, looked decidedly "preppy," and spoke with teacher-like authority. Nothing in his persona would give one the sense that he was attempting to adopt the culture of his students.

Later, I spoke again with some of Mr. Stieber's students. I asked them why they had said he was "really black." They said that he was real, that he was always honest, that he respected his students and insisted that they do their best. One young woman gave an example. She said that she asked Mr. Stieber how he felt as a white man teaching black history. She told me that tears came to his eyes as he answered that when he learned about Emmett Till and other terrible things that white people had done to black people, it sometimes made him ashamed to be white. The student said that tears also came to her eyes, as they connected on a very real level. I found out later that Dave Stieber was deeply involved with a group of African American teachers studying the history of racism in the United States. He had found his mentors and it showed. He shared a work of spoken word poetry with me explicating his reasons for teaching in a school and community that many teachers would shun.

Once again, I do not want to suggest that TFA teachers should disappear. I believe these highly educated, energetic, and often deeply committed young people have a role to play. They can, with humility, under the tutelage of people who look like the children they want to teach, learn to connect with the children they want to reach. If they are mentored by master African American teachers, if they commit to teach long enough to become good at their craft, then they have a lot to offer. They are welcomed and invited in with open arms.

On the other hand, if they enter the classroom arrogantly, believing that young white people like themselves are the saviors of black children, if they ignore the brilliance of many—never to suggest all—of the African American educators who have come before them and who are struggling against all odds to educate the children of their own communities, if they do not understand and work against a belief system that demeans the intelligence of those they purport to help by unquestioningly accepting the idea that school reform means making everything whiter—then they can serve no useful role.

As I reviewed a number of articles on the history of segregation and its consequences to the teaching force, I came across an undated, untitled newspaper article apparently from the seventies that observed, "The more desegregation a state experienced, the fewer black educators they ended up with." In looking at what counts as school reform in most cities in this country, one could easily substitute "school reform" for "desegregation": "The more school reform a state experiences, the fewer black educators they seem to end up with." We must remember that children do need to see and connect to teachers who look like themselves, who know their communities and their lives, who know how to say their names. Whatever else we might do, school reform must include efforts to recruit and sustain local, African American teachers.

If we are serious about democracy, if we are serious about providing equal opportunity for all citizens, if we are serious about equity and justice, then we have to undo any model that obliquely serves to replicate a racist past.

PART THREE
TEACHING ADOLESCENTS

7
PICKING UP THE BROOM:
DEMANDING CRITICAL THINKING

The reductionism that is proliferating in classrooms where low-income children of color spend their days is alarming. In the name of "test prep," students spend hours and hours completing worksheets that are presumably meant to increase their test scores on standardized tests. My own work, unfortunately, has even been used by some program designers or their advocates (whose reading comprehension is apparently very limited!) to justify their mind-numbing practices. Some instructional approaches focused solely on repetition of decontextualized bits may "work" temporarily to raise test scores for children in urban settings, but if the children's minds are not engaged, then the programs are failures.

There are times when students, overexposed to worksheets and minimal thinking, resist being pushed to think. It is as if they have reached an agreement with their teachers—don't ask much of me and I won't make any problems for you. Thus, the "busy-ness" of seat work allows for the appearance of the "control" that many schools in poor communities ask of their teachers, whether any learning is occurring or not. Martin Haberman calls this agreement one aspect of the "pedagogy of poverty."[1] When teachers feel they cannot control a class, they frequently resort to inane seat work: copy all of the "m" words in the dictionary. Students may reward this teacher behavior with compliance and quiet, but they will complain later that the teacher did not care enough to push them. Although they resist, they often want, need, and expect the teacher to push them beyond their comfort zone, and to continue pushing despite their resistance.

Some of the mind-numbing "busy-ness" of low-income school classrooms cannot even be easily related to improving test results. I have seen much too much of what author and educator Mike Schmoker terms the "Crayola Curriculum."[2] When Kati Haycock and her team from the Education Trust visited classrooms, they found that "coloring was *the single most predominant activity* in the schools they had observed—right up through middle school."[3] After Schmoker wrote, "with trepidation," an essay on the phenomenon, he expected to receive an onslaught of negative opinion but instead received an avalanche of letters validating his observations. Not one writer disagreed with his perceptions.[4]

In a recent visit to a social studies class of over-age high schoolers, I walked around the room to talk to students about their seat work. One young man was obviously trying to shield his paper from my view. I tried to coax him to let me see it, but he would not. When I was on the other side of the room he placed the paper, face down, on an empty desk. Later, after the period was over, I stealthily took a look at the paper, thinking I would find a note or even a story he didn't want to share. What I discovered instead saddened me profoundly: a coloring sheet of a turkey, which he had begun to color with different colored pens. There were other such sheets on the teacher's desk. He knew that what he had been asked/allowed to do was infantile, and he was ashamed that anyone would be a witness to it. The saddest part about my visit was that every over-age student I talked to—all of whom had enrolled in this school to complete high school at an accelerated pace—told me that she or he wanted to go to college. From what I saw of the curriculum, it would be a miracle if any made it.

In "Yes We Can: Telling Truths and Dispelling Myths About Race and Education in America," the Education Trust illustrated the disparity in assignments in schools with different demographics. They looked at seventh-grade classrooms in two different California schools, one predominantly white and one predominantly African American and Latino. In the predominantly white school, a typical assignment asked the students to write an essay on Anne Frank. The directions were as follows:

> Your essay will consist of an opening paragraph which introduces the title, author and general background of the novel. Your thesis will state specifically what Anne's overall personality is, and what general psychological and intellectual changes she exhibits over the course of the book. You might organize your essay by grouping psychological and intellectual changes OR you might choose 3 or 4 characteristics (like friendliness, patience, optimism, self doubt) and show how she changes in this area.

An example of a writing assignment the seventh graders in the African American and Latino school typically got was a worksheet: "The 'Me' Page." Students were asked to fill in blanks with one or two words: "my best friend," "a chore I hate," "a car I want," "my heartthrob." The authors add, "given the sort of educational malpractice that our students endure, is it any wonder that achievement gaps have persisted for generations in this country?"[5]

What does it look like to demand critical thinking in classrooms serving low-income students of color? A Native Alaskan teacher recounted to me a favorite story about her own schooling, which provided this teacher with the perspective she needed to teach her students in her own village. She says that her one Native teacher in a high school with a population of all Native students and otherwise white teachers once placed a broom on the floor of the classroom. As the students entered class, they all stepped around or over the broom. After all the students were seated, the teacher picked up the broom and began to lecture them. Why didn't any of them pick the broom up? Did they think it belonged on the floor? Who were they waiting for to tell them what was right? The message of the lesson was contained in her repeated words, "You cannot afford not to think! You cannot wait for others to tell you what you know is right! You have to think! No one will think for you, and if they do, they mean you no good!" This teacher understood that students who are members of a group stigmatized and oppressed by the larger society *have* to learn to think for themselves. Otherwise, they will forever be victims of that society's whims.

A few years ago, I visited with a group of young men enrolled in the Hartford, Connecticut, all-male Benjamin E. Mays Institute, a charter school with an Afrocentric focus. The students were attending a conference where I was to speak. The young middle school men were impressive in their assigned roles of reporting on the conference, taking photographs, and providing necessary set-ups for presenters. I finagled a few minutes to talk with a group of them about their school. Curious about their take on the curriculum, I asked how their school was different from regular public school. One responded that it was different because it was Afrocentric. "What does that mean?" I asked. "It means that we learn how to think for ourselves." Intrigued, I inquired further. "Well," one replied, "in regular public school you just take what the book says as the truth. Here we can question what the book says or what the teachers say, as long as we have a good argument." "Yeah, we have to think," added another. "We know that the book isn't always right. We have to look at a lot of sources, not

just one book." That is one aspect of the kind of critical thinking
I am advocating.

Bill Bigelow has written of his work with teaching partner
Linda Christensen in classrooms of low-income children of color.[6]
Reminiscent of the Freedom School curriculum discussed in
Chapter 2, Bill and Linda invite students to critique the larger society through sharing their lives. In their Literature in U.S. History
course, they use historical concepts as a starting point to explore
themes in students' own lives, and then use students' lives to explore history and current society. In one series of lessons, the class
studied the forced Cherokee Indian removal through role-playing.
As different students portrayed Indians, plantation owners, bank-
ers, and members of the Andrew Jackson administration, they
came to understand more deeply the forces that combined to push
the Cherokees west against their will. After discussions of how and
why this happened, the teachers asked the students to write about
a time when they had had their rights violated. Students were to
write "from inside" these experiences to capture what they felt at
the time and what, if anything, they did about the injustice.

Students shared the writings in a circle: one spoke of how she
wet her pants because the teacher wouldn't let her go to the bathroom; another talked about a middle school teacher who "leched
after the girls"; another about being sexually harassed on her walk
to school and then being mistreated by the school administration when she reported the incident. Students were asked to make
notes about the "collective text" when they read individual stories.
They spent class time reviewing their notes, analyzing their stories,
and looking for themes. They were surprised at how little resistance each student had mounted as a result of the injustice and
were thus presumably more able to understand the frequent lack
of resistance in historical injustices and the phenomenal courage
present when organized resistance is mounted.

Bigelow writes:

> Our broader objective was to search for social meaning in individual experience—to push students to use their stories as windows not only on their lives, but on society. . . . One function of the school curriculum is to celebrate the culture of the dominant group and to ignore or scorn the culture of subordinate groups. The personal writing, collective texts, and discussion circles . . . are attempts to challenge students not to accept these judgments [and] . . . to grasp that they can create knowledge and not simply absorb it from higher authorities.[7]

Bigelow cautions that everything was not neat and easy in their classroom. All the students did not immediately embrace this kind of instruction (one is quoted as saying, "Why do we have to have all this personal stuff? Can't you just give us a book or a worksheet and leave us alone?"), but most did become engaged. The teachers, always involved in their own critical thinking and assessments, used students' dissenting comments to constantly analyze, revise, and refine their lessons.[8]

The urgent need for demanding critical thinking of our students exists in all subject areas. Only those who are authentically and critically literate can become the independently thinking citizens required for any society's evolution. The opportunity to achieve such levels of literacy is even more critical for those whom the larger society stigmatizes. The comments of Carter G. Woodson in *The Miseducation of the Negro* in 1933 give us something to ponder in today's educational milieu. When people of color are taught to accept uncritically texts and histories that reinforce their marginalized position in society, they easily learn never to question their position:

> Taught the same economics, history, philosophy, literature and religion which have established the present code of morals, the

Negro's mind has been brought under the control of his oppressor. The problem of holding the Negro down, therefore, is easily solved. When you control a man's thinking you do not have to worry about his actions. You do not have to tell him not to stand here or go yonder. He will find his "proper place" and will stay in it. You do not need to send him to the back door. He will go without being told. In fact, if there is no back door, he will cut one for his special benefit. His education makes it necessary.[9]

Yet, most of the literacy instruction provided in schools for low-income students is not only uncritical, it is often virtually nonexistent. Most would argue that literacy is the ability to read and write. One would assume, therefore, that much of the instruction in schools would focus on one or the other skill. Instead, what typically happens is what Dick Allington calls "stuff" and Lucy Calkins refers to as "literacy based arts and crafts."[10] Allington and his colleagues found that struggling readers spent many hours on certain workbook activities, despite persistent research evidence that such activities were actually harmful to literacy development.[11] Mike Schmoker cites Elaine McEwan, a well-known educator, who describes elementary students who spent thirty-seven hours—the equivalent of an entire month of language arts—building a papier-mâché dinosaur. "Those kids," says McEwan, "couldn't read well, but they spent all that time messing with chicken wire and wheat paste."[12] This is not to say that the arts have no role in literacy education or critical thinking. In many classrooms, students use the arts as a basis for reading and writing. They research particular artists, discuss their styles, and debate the elements necessary to reproduce aspects of the artists' work. Other teachers use music to inspire creative writing. Still others have students analyze and discuss text in order to create masks to represent the different characters in a play. Students must defend their choices with references to both the direct text and the implied meanings.

What does work, whether using the arts as a basis or not, is having kids read, write, and discuss text. Surprisingly, those activities are seldom seen in classrooms of low-performing, low-income schools.[13] If we did less unrelated "stuff" and more actual reading and discussing of reading, our students would have the opportunity to excel. Kati Haycock has calculated that *three to four weeks* of effective, full-day literacy instruction would allow the average student to gain *an entire year* of academic growth.[14]

The consensus of researchers and practitioners is that spending time reading, discussing, and writing about text *in class* allows students to become crucially literate. Too often teachers assign readings for homework, while at the same time complaining that low-performing students don't do homework! Students who need help reading, need considerable help interpreting texts. There are too many sources for interactive reading strategies that aid comprehension to cite here, but a simple Internet search would uncover multitudes. The problem is, because our students don't typically read in the classroom, we don't use them.

A part of the critical literacy development our young people need comes from open-ended discussion of important themes. In the Learning 24/7 study, researchers found evidence of academic dialogue and discussion in only 0.05 percent of the fifteen hundred classes they observed. Without discussions, students are left to maneuver their way through unfamiliar territory with no support. Engaging in deep discussions of text across subject areas can, as in Bill Bigelow's class, connect text to young people's lives, which in turn will also tie them more intimately to the text.

A few years ago I visited the Carter G. Woodson Charter Middle School in Chicago. The students are African American, the teachers more diverse, and the principal and vice-principal are African American men who also teach. Depending on the year, 75 to 85 percent of the students qualify for free or reduced-price lunch. Enrollment is open to all, with a lottery determining placement when there are more applicants than spaces.

The teachers do not teach to the test. Students learn in a variety of settings, including learning to make films, doing art work connected to academic goals, and having poetry slams. Every child, no matter his or her scores on standardized tests, must participate in activities beyond paper-and-pencil classroom work, including involvement in the community-based organization Digital Youth Network, which states as its goal preparing students to be reflective and critical thinkers who are committed to personal and community improvement.

Every child completes a "Signature Project" individually or in a group. These projects are integrated in some form into the students' regular studies. Two seventh graders shared their project with me when I visited—a video on the roots of Chicago jazz. The students located the film's archival pictures, researched the history, located the music for the soundtrack, and conducted the interviews on their own. They had to write and discuss papers about their findings. The results were phenomenal. They also discussed ideas for exploring additional questions and refining their work as they continued to work on the project during their eighth-grade year.

I also visited a seventh-grade classroom where the students were discussing the book *Monster* by Walter Dean Myers. The book is a series of reflections and interviews with a young African American man who is in prison for murder. They had read the book in class and were now listening to a taped extract. After listening, the teacher had the students divide up into small groups—a task, evidenced by the speed with which they accomplished it, with which that they were quite familiar. The students were to discuss the question, "Is Adolfo (the main character) a monster or is he not?" The discussion was lively, with students arguing their points of view with great energy. The teacher continued to remind them as they argued, "I want to hear evidence-based information about your opinion!"

Most groups said the main character was not a monster, but a victim of his circumstances—a drug-addicted mother, poverty, bad luck, etc. They referred to the text to support their opinions. One boy had remained quiet. The teacher called on him: "Well, I think he is a monster, because my mother was a drug addict when I was seven years old and I was poor. I decided to go to friends' mothers and other relatives for help. I made the decision that I could be different. It's all about the choices you make!" He gave everyone something to think about. The teacher did not wrap up the discussion with "the right answer," but allowed the varying perspectives to remain as possibilities. The teacher told me later that she also used these discussions to encourage students to connect the reading of one book with others they would study.

Aside from the energy, enthusiasm, and clear opportunity to engage in the text with critical thinking, it is also interesting to note the level of social support that existed in the classroom. There are not too many school settings in which students feel comfortable enough to share the difficult and deeply personal information that the young man quoted above shared.

Another example of a teacher who demands critical thinking with extraordinary results is Dr. Abdulahim Shabazz, who, at three historically black universities, has successfully taught students who came to college with severe deficits in mathematics. During 1956–1963, while he was chair of the Mathematics Department at Atlanta University, 109 students graduated with master's degrees in math. More than one-third of those went on to earn doctorates in mathematics or math education from some of the best universities in the United States. Nearly 50 percent of the African American PhD mathematicians in 1990 in the United States (about two hundred) resulted in some way from the original 109 Shabazz master's students.[15] Shabazz says that a significant percentage of the original 109 began with serious academic deficits in math and language arts. His slogan has always been,

"Give me your worst ones and I will teach them." How has he done this?

In an interview with Dr. Asa Hilliard, Shabazz made it clear that SAT and ACT scores have almost no meaning for him, but that he has focused on a set of excellence-level goals that have shaped his approach to dealing with all students. His goals are:

- to teach understanding rather than merely to teach mathematical operations;
- to teach mathematical language for the purpose of communicating with mathematics and not merely as a way to solve textbook problems;
- to teach his students that math is not at all a fixed body of knowledge but that it is an experimental enterprise in the truest sense of that word and that their approach to the solution of mathematical problems then and in the future should be to try a variety of strategies;
- to have students believe, as he does, that mathematics "is nothing more than a reflection of life and that life itself is mathematical," and he wants them to know that the symbols used in mathematics approximate the reality of human experience and cosmic operations; and
- to give his students a sense of hope that they can become superior performers.[16]

This is a testament to demanding critical thinking, not accepting anything as a given, understanding one's own agency in the process of education, and connecting teaching and learning to the students' own worlds. Other successful teachers have adopted various versions of this thinking strategy to their own subject areas and to varying ages of students.

Educator Martin Haberman asks whether it is possible to describe a learning environment that, rather than replicating a "pedagogy of poverty," instead promotes real learning in urban schools. His list of what that environment might look like, I believe, reflects what Abdulahim Shabazz, Bill Bigelow and Linda Christensen, the teachers at Carter G. Woodson, and other teachers who demand critical thinking of their charges do regularly:

- Whenever students are involved with issues they regard as vital concerns, good teaching is going on.
- Whenever students are involved with explanations of human differences, good teaching is going on.
- Whenever students are being helped to see major concepts, big ideas, and general principles and are not merely engaged in the pursuit of isolated facts, good teaching is going on.
- Whenever students are involved in planning what they will be doing, it is likely that good teaching is going on.
- Whenever students are involved with applying ideas such as fairness, equity, or justice to their world, it is likely that good teaching is going on.
- Whenever students are actively involved, it is likely that good teaching is going on.
- Whenever students are directly involved in a real-life experience, it is likely that good teaching is going on.
- Whenever students are actively involved in heterogeneous groups, it is likely that good teaching is going on.
- Whenever students are asked to think about an idea in a way that questions common sense or a widely accepted assumption that relates new ideas to ones learned previously or that applies an idea to the problems of living, then there is a good chance that good teaching is going on.
- Whenever students are involved in reading, polishing, or perfecting their work, it is likely that good teaching is going on.

- Whenever teachers involve students with the technology of information access, good teaching is going on.
- Whenever students are involved in reflecting on their own lives and how they have come to believe and feel as they do, good teaching is going on.[17]

Although we sometimes seem to act to the contrary, there is no real dichotomy between teaching "basic skills" and insisting that children learn to think critically. When we teach appropriate conventions and strategies within the context of critical thinking, we can produce the educated people we strive for.

8
HOW WOULD A FOOL DO IT?
ASSESSMENT

Psychologist Michael Cole and his colleagues once attempted to assess the IQ of some Kpelle tribesmen of Liberia with the WISC test of intelligence, which uses pictures instead of words. Correct responses would have the test takers group pictures into categories—containers, tools, and food. Over and over, the Kpelle test takers would pair a potato with a knife "because you cut potatoes with a knife," and a basket with vegetables because, of course, "you carry vegetables in a basket." In frustration, the researchers asked, "Is there any other way to do it?" They always got the same response: "That is how a wise man would do it." Finally, one of the researchers asked, "Well, how would a fool do it?" The Kpelle immediately placed the pictures in what the WISC deemed the "right" categories![1]

Assessment is a lot trickier than we think, especially if the children we are assessing are not from the same culture as the test makers. We may be able to get some gross measures, such as whether a child knows his or her alphabet or whether he or she can divide. Even these measures may prove problematic if we are dealing with decontextualized assessments. I will never forget my six-year-old student, many years ago, whom I could not get, despite all my efforts, to successfully complete worksheets on coins and their values. When I got to know this little boy better, I found out that he was perfectly knowledgeable about using coins, making change, and paying for items with ease. He could do money, he just couldn't do *worksheets* about money!

When a teacher is familiar with aspects of a child's culture, then the teacher may be better able to assess the child's competence. Many teachers, unfamiliar with the language, the metaphors, or the environment of the children they teach may easily underestimate the children's competence.

Wise kindergarten teacher and author Vivian Paley has noted that she probably missed much of the expressed intelligence of her students from another culture. She pointed out that when a child who shared her own Jewish background made comments about meat and dairy dishes, she received instant messages about his or her intelligence. But when several African American children told her that "black people don't eat pig; only white people eat pig," she was honestly insightful enough to admit that she may have been missing part of the intellectual picture presented by not being familiar with the context within which black children made simple statements.[2]

A professor at a local, predominantly white university invited me to speak to her early childhood education students. In preparation for the visit, the professor asked the students to write anonymously about their experiences with urban children. One very thoughtful young white woman wrote about her experience as one of the only four white adults in an urban preschool setting. She realized that the preschool knowledge and experiences she took for granted were not shared by these preschoolers. Instead of more familiar themes, the dramatic play corner often involved someone being taken away to jail. After reading the children's book *The Mitten*, the head teacher asked the children what other things they might wear when it was cold outside. One student raised his hand and answered "handcuffs." After an initial chuckle, the young teacher realized that the child probably knew someone who had been publicly arrested during a cold weather spell, and so the child equated the cold with handcuffs. The teacher went on to comment that the surrounding neighborhood, and even the school playground, were often filled with police cars. One four-year-old responded to seeing a police car by walking toward it saying, "I ain't afraid of no po-po!" using a popular neighborhood term for the police.

Would many teachers be able to recognize the intelligence or even the meaning underlying these students' comments? Or would they just shake their heads at the "violent homes and communities" of their students and question whether they would be able to teach them anything? A lack of knowledge and understanding of students' out-of-school experiences severely limit a teacher's ability to see his or her students' intelligence and problem-solving skills and may feed stereotypes about the educability of the children in the classroom.

I continue to be charmed by the response to an assessment by another African American preschooler. In her seminal book about the culturally influenced language patterns of three communities, *Ways with Words*, Shirley Brice Heath tells of working with two- to four-year-old black children to determine their categorization skills. She placed a box and a number of plastic forks of different sizes on the table. She then held up a fork and asked the children to put all the forks that were like the one she held into the box. She expected that the children would attend to the size of the fork. They did everything but. One noticed a blue streak in the plastic of the one she held and proceeded to put the forks that had similar coloration in the box. Others spread the forks all over the table. Others created their own game of the forks. Finally, she told one little boy that he needed to play her game. "Why?" he asked, "Who make you do dis?"[3] In other words, why would anyone voluntarily engage in such uninteresting behavior? So much for getting some children to participate in research or assessments that they find purposeless!

Yet, in schools, these children would not be viewed as creative or thoughtful but merely unable to do the task. Accurately monitoring and assessing children means being able to go deep into their thinking, to figure out not only the "correctness" or "incorrectness" of an answer but the thinking that led to it. It is an understanding of the thought process that will inform teaching more than any answer sheet. I am reminded of a young teenager who always scored poorly on history tests. The teacher's "help" was to tell her she needed to read more carefully for the "main idea" of a passage. The student explained her dilemma to me: "Well, she wants to know the main idea of this paragraph about Lincoln. She says the main idea is why he had to lead the nation in a Civil War. When I read it, it talked about him being depressed, and I think that's the main idea, because if he was depressed he might not be able to think of other alternatives!" Good point. The teacher did not understand the thinking of this wise child, only that she got the answer "wrong."

The "main idea" of a passage is merely someone's interpretation of the author's intention. Author Wayne Dyer says he once applied for a job assessing student test papers. He had to take the test himself before he could get the job and was surprised to see a passage from one of his own books on the test. When he got back the results, it was a bit of a shock to find that he had gotten the question regarding "the main idea" of the passage he had authored wrong.[4]

A skilled young Latina teacher, Ms. Rodriguez, helped her students gain an understanding of scoring well on standardized writing assessments by discussing with them who would be grading their writing. These diverse Florida middle school students evaluated each other's writing by adopting the perspective of, as Ms.

Rodriguez called them, "the little white ladies in Tallahassee!" (a reference to the assessors in the state's capital).[5] That made the assessment of their writing not a question of right or wrong but of appropriateness for the potential assessors.

What Can Teachers Do?

How can individual teachers know all that they need to know to accurately monitor and assess children from cultures other than their own? The easy answer is that they can't. This kind of knowledge is best gleaned from teams of preferably diverse teachers who collaborate around teaching and learning. Hilliard relates that many people believe that teachers should collaborate to find the magic bullet that will allow them to become more effective. He counters that collaboration apparently *is* the magic bullet.[6]

My favorite work on creating collaboration through developing professional learning communities is Mike Schmoker's *Results Now*. The core argument of Schmoker's book is that we know two things that can provide us with a monumentally historic opportunity to improve schools:

1. Instruction itself has the largest influence on achievement (a fact still dimly acknowledged).
2. Most (though not all) instruction, despite our best intentions, is not effective but could improve significantly and swiftly through ordinary and accessible arrangements among teachers and administrators.[7]

Schmoker lists a set of essential teaching practices for which he believes schools do not currently require teachers to be accountable:

+ being clear about what is to be learned and assessed;

- using assessments to evaluate a lesson's effectiveness and making constructive adjustments on the basis of results;
- conducting a check for understanding at certain points in the lesson;
- having kids read for higher-order purposes and write regularly;
- clearly explicating and carefully teaching the criteria by which student work will be scored or evaluated.[8]

His solution for ensuring the implementation of these essential practices, now echoed by others in the field, is the creation of teams of teachers who will work together in "professional learning communities." The work of these communities is to establish a common, concise set of what they believe to be essential standards and to teach them in roughly common time frames. He suggests that teams of teachers (teams being based on subject areas for secondary or grade level for elementary) consult their state assessment guides and other documents to help them make the best decisions about what to teach or not teach. He adds that teams must meet regularly—at least twice a month for forty-five minutes or longer. In these meetings, teachers help each other develop and assess lessons that teach to the standards. The time should be totally focused on talking about and analyzing precisely and concretely the results achieved with specific lessons and units.

In order to accomplish this work, Schmoker adds that teachers must develop and make frequent use of short-term common assessments. With common assessments, teachers can engage in active or practitioner research.[9] I would add that in schools trying to raise the achievement levels of students from diverse backgrounds, conversations about culture and the knowledge students bring with them should be part of lesson development. Thus, no one teacher is asked to know everything about the children being taught, but the collective knowledge can be pooled for more effective lesson development. Further, when teachers realize that there is something they do not know about their students, they can plan to explore it collectively.

In a recent in-service with teachers at a high school serving low-income African American students, I asked the teachers to make lists of the strengths and challenges the school faced in its endeavors to improve achievement. One of the challenges was poor attendance. We discussed why the teachers thought the attendance was low, and each had some small piece of an explanation. They realized that one thing that had never happened in their school was posing that question to the students. The teachers decided, as a group, that part of the math curriculum at the beginning of the year would be involving students in a research study to ask other students why the attendance was so low. Analyzing the data would be a part of the students' curriculum, and the teachers would use the results in rethinking their school practices. I don't know whether their plan worked to reduce absenteeism, but if they continued this model for collaborative problem solving, I have no doubt that they eventually found a solution.

Instead of the American "drop in to hear the expert" model of staff development, Japan utilizes a model similar to the one described above. Teams of teachers work together to analyze student assessments and then craft and refine lessons and units until they have achieved an optimal effect on student learning. Refined and tested lessons are then made available to all teachers. In their book *The Teaching Gap*, James Stigler and James Hiebert looked at teaching in Germany, Japan, and the United States. They found that American teachers were good at implementing American teaching methods, but it was the methods themselves that were flawed.[10] Other countries are continually improving their teaching, but the United States has no mechanism in place to do so. Adopting a model more akin to that used in Japan and Germany would give U.S. schools a teacher-led process for assessing and improving classroom instruction.

A very successful, all-day in-service I recently attended at a middle school was completely run by teachers. They spent the first part of the day looking at student performance data from teacher assessments and from state-mandated assessments in groups of two or three. They made decisions about how they needed to adjust instruction based on their analyses of student data. Later in the day, one of the teachers presented for the rest of the faculty his research on improving achievement for low-income students. His presentation was "hands on" and involved, again, pooling the knowledge of all those present.

Schmoker emphasizes the need to create "short-term wins" by looking for monthly gains rather than just focusing on larger, high-stakes tests. He describes the successes of several schools that have developed such a focus. Peck Elementary in Colorado, for example, saw monthly gains in specific areas of math and literacy well before they saw sizeable annual improvement on the state's assessment test. Another example Schmoker cites is Donaldson Elementary School in Arizona, where a powerful lesson plan that a group of teachers created in just fifteen minutes produced an increase in students' ability to write effective "descriptive settings" from 4 in 88 students to 85 in 88 students in one month.[11]

Too often in schools, we either ask teachers to be lone rangers in trying to create better instruction, or we give them prescribed "teacher-proof" lessons that may or may not be appropriate for their students. In any case, the predeveloped lessons cause a kind of dependency that can encourage teachers to disengage from the results of their teaching—"I did what they said and if it didn't work, it's not my fault." I believe that if we give teachers the tools and opportunity to collaborate and hold them accountable for their results, we can ensure that they are invested in what they are teaching, and we can improve instruction, the monitoring of student work, and culturally sensitive assessment.

Furthermore, those teachers who create high performance in their classrooms usually remain as isolated as those who consistently produce low performance. The creation of focused, collaborative professional learning environments can help make high performance more widespread and help lower-performing teachers develop the knowledge and skills to improve their practice.

Frequently, when I have suggested rethinking instruction and assessment to teachers, they have rolled their eyes as they lament the state-mandated standards or curricula. One district supervisor said to me that she used to tell teachers, "Teach what you love." Now she tells them, admittedly somewhat facetiously, "Love the curriculum!" The reality is that most of the mandated curricula I have looked at are not terrible. Many lessons are quite good, even if the entire curriculum seems to try to include much too much information to focus effectively. If nothing else, they give us a basis to work from in determining a scope and sequence, as well as a vehicle to begin collaboration. I remember being delighted as a new teacher many years ago to find stuffed into the back of a closet a curriculum guide for my grade that included a scope and sequence. Because I was teaching during the "open classroom, teach-what-you-want era," I had no idea of what my second graders were expected to know. This guide helped me immensely in developing lessons that better prepared my charges for their future.

Some administrators are now realizing that we must focus test-centered teaching as much as possible. Instead of trying to teach every standard and every lesson, they get sample copies of the state tests so teachers can see what standards the tests actually emphasize. No test actually addresses all standards, and some are assessed more deeply than others. No matter what the standards dictate, there is plenty of room for teachers working together to refine mandated instruction so that it is more appropriate for their students. Such an approach also provides more time for the development of creative units that excite teachers and address student interests. If we can begin the team process at all schools in a district, perhaps this will be the beginning of an opportunity for practicing teachers to create curriculum collectively rather than depending on so-called experts.

It is important to mention here that, although many schools now have what they call "professional learning communities," these are not really focused on teachers collectively solving problems. In some schools, teachers just meet together to report on what they are doing. In others, grade-level housekeeping tasks are addressed. It is not easy to develop a collaborative spirit when teachers have been isolated for so long, so explicit attention must be given to collaboration if it is to really occur. I am currently involved with one school as it participates in the National Board for Professional Teaching Standards' new Take One! program in which all the teachers in a school work on one element of board certification. The program is designed to ensure that teachers work collaboratively to study each other's videotaped classroom lessons and identify means to improve the content and lesson delivery. Although we are only beginning the process, I believe that this program may allow an accelerated path to developing real professional learning communities within schools.

Teacher Assessment

In teacher assessment as well as in student assessment, we have to address the barrier of different cultures placing different meanings on the same behavior. I was involved in the early development of assessment protocols for the National Board of Professional Teaching Standards at Stanford University. In trying to develop initial prototypes for various ways they might assess teachers, the

Stanford researchers assembled a group of high school kids from Palo Alto, near Stanford—very well-to-do kids—and filmed a number of teachers instructing the students. A group of assessors rated the teachers' performances.

One of the teachers on that video was an African American male. The lesson was on the causes of the Civil War. The African American teacher started the lesson by asking the students about themselves, about their lives, about their schools, and so forth. Then he told a condensed story of the Civil War in its entirety. While telling the story he would occasionally stop to ask the students personal questions. The assessors complained, first of all, that he lectured too much, that he was trying to talk about too much, and that he was disorganized. Then they went on to criticize him for repeatedly stopping his lesson and asking personal questions. (When one of the researchers interviewed this teacher afterwards, he said that he was attempting to get to know the students because, "I can't teach you unless I know you, so I have to have a personal connection." He also said that with the students he usually taught, he had to tell the whole story of an event to get them interested in the details.)

Another teacher on the video was a white male teacher. He had the same group of students and also taught a lesson on the Civil War. He divided the students into groups and gave each group a problem to solve related to determining what led up to the Civil War. He assigned each student a role in the group—"you're the national government, you're the state, you're the state governor, you're the legislature"—and asked each to discuss how he or she would solve the problem. He sat on the side, on a window ledge, while the students all tried to solve their respective problems. He was given much higher marks by the assessors.

Interestingly, a colleague of mine then showed the videos of the two teachers to a group of students in Roxbury, an African American community in Boston. She asked the students to assess the two teachers. Their assessment was that the black teacher was a "real teacher"; he cared about his students; he was really teaching. The white teacher wasn't even teaching; he was lazy; he didn't care about his students; he was just sitting over there on the window sill. The point is not that all classes for African American students should be lectures or structured in the way the African American teacher taught but that we need to understand that the initial interpretation of different kinds of teaching behaviors may stand in the way of getting across the messages that we want to transmit to students.

Assessment is considerably more complex than what can be gleaned from paper-and-pencil tests. Even observations are suspect when those doing the observing are not familiar with the culture of those being observed. There is no simple solution to the problem, but when both instruction and assessment depend on the collective knowledge of teachers, when lessons and evaluation instruments are reinvented by constantly considering what works and what doesn't work, when educators thoughtfully work together to improve each other's abilities, then we have the best chance of creating schools that provide the best possible education for all students.

9

SHOOTING HOOPS:
WHAT CAN WE LEARN
ABOUT THE DRIVE FOR EXCELLENCE?

Imagine a little black boy, like millions around the country, who goes out to the local playground after school to shoot hoops. The first time he goes out, he shoots twenty times and misses twenty times. Still, he comes back every day. The next week he might make a few baskets. After a few months of daily attempts, some days he makes seven or even ten out of twenty. Other days, he makes only three. After a year or so, he makes many more shots than he misses. Despite week after week of relative failure, he continues to try, until he eventually finds success.

There are two questions I find important to ask about this behavior. One question is fairly easy to answer. The second question, which I will pose later, is more complex but absolutely critical to improving our work in schools.

The first question, the simpler one to answer, is why did the boy become better? Yes, the answer, of course, is practice. But the concept of practice includes some deeper layers that require further exploration. We've been trained to believe that talent is something we are born with, that it comes in the genes. In fact, in schools we seem to believe that people are born into three categories of talent—low, average, and high—and that it is our primary job to find students' "correct" category and act with diligence to ensure that they stay in it.

The notion of ability or talent set in stone at the moment of conception has actually been brought into question through both statistical research and careful scrutiny of the life paths of exceptionally talented individuals. True, some might have some inborn advantage in some areas over others. What drives excellence, however, is not solely genes but a combination of innate ability, cultural environment, drive, and practice. And of these, practice and the belief that practicing hard will improve performance seem to top the list. This appears to hold true in a multitude of arenas, from sports to music to tested IQ.

David Shenk, in his innovative book *The Genius in All of Us*, provides several examples, including Michael Jordan, a perfect case study. Without doubt, Jordan is the epitome of a sports legend. He could leap so far to the hoop and remain airborne for so long that it looked as if he could actually defy gravity: thus, "Air Jordan." He could also "move, shoot, pass, defend, and dunk so much better than any other player that he took on a superhuman aura," says Shenk.[1] Renowned basketball coach Phil Jackson called Jordan "pure genius."[2]

But this pure genius was nowhere to be found when Jordan was young. He was not even the best athlete in his family—older brother Larry was. He was not the hardest worker; he actually had the reputation of being the laziest of his five siblings. In fact, after attending summer basketball camp, Jordan didn't even make the varsity basketball squad in high school.

One thing about Michael, though, he hated losing. And he got a lot of practice losing when he played his brother Larry. But when

Michael was cut from the varsity team in the tenth grade while his friend Roy Smith made it, something apparently happened to Michael. His sense of drive kicked in and seemed to create a willingness to do absolutely anything to improve his skills. For the remainder of his basketball career, no one ever practiced so long or played so hard. The rest is history. Jordan was not "born" with skills that he exhibited from childhood. He developed the skills through his drive and willingness to put in those countless hours of practice.

Many who believe that people are born with or without musical talent, point a finger to Beethoven, Mozart, or YoYo Ma. The reality is that in each of these and other cases of musical genius, while we cannot determine what their genes held, the extraordinary talent came from exposure to a musical environment and practice, practice, and more practice.

In all cases, their extraordinary ability came only after years of intensive work—and in the case of Beethoven, after horrific abuse. Here is one description of Beethoven's childhood from Edmund Morris's biography:

> Neighbors of the Beethovens . . . recall seeing a small boy "standing in front of the clavier and weeping." He was so short he had to climb a footstool to reach the keys. If he hesitated, his father beat him. When he was allowed off, it was only to have a violin thrust into his hands, or musical theory drummed into his head. There were few days when he was not flogged, or locked up in the cellar. [His father] also deprived him of sleep, waking him at midnight for more hours of practice.[3]

Innate ability or practice?

Shinichi Suzuki, famed educator and violin teacher who taught even very young children to play the violin, did not concern himself with capacity or ability. He developed a method of instruction that assumed that all children had the capacity to learn to play the violin. And all the children he and those who followed his methods taught, learned to play and learned to play well. In Suzuki's words, "Musical ability is not an inborn talent but an ability which must be developed. Any child who is properly trained can develop musical ability, just as all children develop the ability to speak their mother tongue. The potential of every child is unlimited."[4]

Another aspect of human ability that we have been led to believe is innate is how one scores on IQ tests. A number of studies have disproved this notion, but none more interestingly than a study led by Eleanor Maguire in 1999 in which spatial intelligence as an inborn ability (as measured by IQ tests) was completely discredited.

Maguire studied spatial ability by comparing the brains of London cabbies with those of non–cab drivers. The knowledge that London cab drivers must acquire is extraordinarily complicated. The streets of London are some of the most intricate in the world. "Within a six-mile radius of Charing Cross Station, some twenty-five thousand streets connect and bisect at every possible angle, dead-ending into parks, monuments, shops and private homes." In order to become properly licensed, London taxi drivers must learn all of these driving nooks and crannies, an encyclopedic awareness known proudly in the trade as 'The Knowledge.'"[5]

Maguire did MRIs on the brains of London cabbies and compared them with those of non-cabbies. In contrast with the non-cabbies, experienced taxi drivers had a greatly enlarged posterior hippocampus—the part of the brain that specializes in recalling spatial representations. One might argue that the difference might be accounted for by the tendency of those with a more developed posterior hippocampus to choose taxi driving. An additional discovery, however, discounts that argument: The longer the cabbies had been working, *the larger that part of the brain was.*

This finding shows that not only ability but the actual brain structure was changed as a result of an environment that required practicing a skill. Further, this change happened in adulthood and was not something that these cabbies were born with. Not only was spatial intelligence an acquired skill but the *adult* brain could be molded as a result of practice and drive. This is a true indication of the brain's "plasticity." In other words, every human brain has the built-in capacity to become, over time, what we demand of it. No ability is fixed. Practice can even change the brain.

This discussion explains why the "basketball boy" gets better— he practices. It also explains why people get better at everything— they practice. When we encounter children in our classes who are not performing, the likely culprit is *not* that they do not have the innate ability or the capacity to accomplish the tasks, the reality is that they have not engaged in sufficient practice.

The answer might seem simple—ensure that they engage in more practice of school tasks. There is still a problem, however: how do we ensure that they engage in the necessary practice? Many teachers of inner-city children complain about the students' lack of motivation. They say the young people will not try, that as soon as they encounter a problem they give up. So how does a teacher get these unmotivated, fearful-of-failure, unwilling-to-try students to engage in the practice they need to improve their school achievement?

And therein lies the second, and more pertinent, question that the basketball boy's story elicits: Why, in the face of apparent failure, does the boy continue to come back, day after day, week after week, month after month, to improve his shooting abilities? What is it about basketball that makes him so willing to work so hard, to put in the long-term commitment necessary for success?

I have asked this question of a number of audiences of teachers, graduate students, community members, and administrators. Their answers are almost always similar:

- He comes back because it is fun: it is engaging because he uses his mind and his body; he can monitor his own progress, adjusting his attempts to match his assessment; it is connected to his interests.
- He comes back so that he can be a part of a culturally rewarded community activity: he wants to get the praise of his peers; his entire community supports basketball; he wants to fit in.
- He comes back because he believes he can get better: he knows that people who look like him have been successful; he sees this success on television and in his own community.
- He comes back because he believes he might get financially rewarded for getting better: he sees people on television who look like him get high salaries for being good at basketball.

I then ask my audiences how these elements relate to school. Why don't our basketball boys persevere in the classroom? Why do they give up as soon as they encounter any academic difficulty? Their answers always inspire further discussion:

- They don't think school is fun. The students can seldom assess themselves; the teacher is the one who calls all the shots. What they are asked to learn is not connected to their interests.
- The people they most care about—other students— seldom reward them for school efforts. Indeed, they aren't even likely to be rewarded for effort in school unless they excel. Doing well in school might make them less likely to fit in with their peers because there is no collectively embraced "culture of achievement" in schools.
- They don't really believe that they can improve their

school achievement. Most of the people they identify
with aren't achieving either. There are so many stereotypes that say that black people are better at sports than
academics. They don't know or see adults on a regular
basis who are both "cool" and academic achievers.

♦ School achievement is weakly connected in their minds
to financial gain. The people whom they typically connect with school (i.e., teachers) clearly are not very affluent. (One teacher said a student looked at her old car and
said he was planning to go a different direction since he
wanted a Mercedes!)

The next question is the one most critical to our work in
schools: If we want students who engage in the practice necessary
to achieve, if we want students who persist in the face of failure, if
we want students who want to come to school, then what do we
need to do to make school more like basketball?

I propose that the answer to that question can only be revealed
by posing several more questions: First, *are we connecting in positive ways to the culture that our African American young people
bring to school?*

This does not mean turning every lesson into a rap but building on some of the deep cultural gifts that African American children bring to school. One such gift is the culturally embedded and
rewarded notion of caring for others—nurturing younger siblings
and other children. An example I have used in presentations is the
teacher who brings candy to school for some holiday. She puts it on
a tray and passes the tray around, asking children to take one piece
and pass the tray on. Before the tray circulates to all the students,
the candy is gone. The teacher has two response choices. One would
elicit the comment, "I just can't do anything nice for these children.
They don't know how to follow any rules. They are so greedy and
uncaring of others' feelings that they want to take their share and

everyone else's, too." The wise teacher, or the one who aspires to wisdom by consulting culturally knowledgeable others for the answer to the disappearing candy, would come to realize that the children took extra candy, not for themselves, but for siblings at home. These children have been taught that they must not accept anything unless they can share with those at home. Most of us from middle-class homes can rest assured that if our children took extra candy, it was not to share with anyone else but to have extra for themselves!

This notion of sharing, of nurturing, of looking out for others is a cultural strength that could be built upon readily in schools. We can institute peer and cross-age tutoring or have older students write books for younger children explaining scientific or social-science concepts (and of course, if you can explain it in a way that younger children can understand it, then you certainly understand the concept yourself). The highly successful "Young People's Project," a spinoff of the national Algebra Project instituted by Robert Moses, has college students teach math to high school students and then supervise after-school programs in which the high school students create mathematics-based learning environments for elementary and middle school students.

A second question: *Are we ensuring that our students know that people who look like them, both in the past and present, have produced and are producing phenomenal intellectual accomplishments?*

Our young African American students need to know that their ancestors were not merely adept at sports. They must understand the intellectual achievements of ancient Africans in Egypt, Timbuktu, and other parts of Africa so that they can understand at a deep level that they come from brilliance. They must also have the opportunity to learn about current black scholars, doctors, lawyers, social activists, innovators, scientists, mathematicians, entrepreneurs, writers, etc., and have the opportunity to personally meet and work with as many as we can provide. Their school curricula should be filled with the stories of African American genius.

Our children must not only have visions of themselves excelling on the basketball court but in every aspect of human achievement. They must be allowed to see multiple paths to financial security and make role models of real people who have taken those paths.

A third question: *Are we making connections between young people's lives and the content that we attempt to teach? Do they feel welcomed into the school environment, or do they feel that they must change who they are to be accepted?*

Basketball is certainly welcoming to young African American men. In large part, school is not. In an article subtitled "The Plight of African American Male Students Engaged in Educational Exchange Processes," researcher Adair F. White-Johnson tells the tale of five young African American men who left school early. White-Johnson interviewed both the young men and the school's teachers and administrators. It was clear that many teachers felt that if the students' dress or behavior did not match the school's expectations, then there was no reason to try to teach them. Some of the students indicated that there was no way, if they were black, that the teachers viewed them as smart. They did not feel at all welcomed. Several indicated that they felt they "didn't have a chance" in the school. White-Johnson concludes that the students felt they were asked by the educational system to surrender or give up their cultural norms and values to achieve academically. Some acquiesced to the school's demands, but some exhibited resistance to school as a reflection of the resistance they perceived the school exhibited toward them.[6]

This is an all-too-common story of black males and schools. How can we change the dynamic so that young African Americans feel that school is the place for them—and for their interests, their hopes, their concerns, and their communities?

Alfred Tatum, author of several books on the topic, recently wrote an article in *Educational Leadership* titled "Engaging African American Males in Reading." Tatum argues that none of the new reforms, new reading series, new accountability structures, or new teachers will make any difference as long as we do not present a new curriculum—and in the context of literacy, new texts—connected to the lives and aspirations of young African Americans.

Tatum contends that by selecting the right reading material teachers can connect African American adolescent males with text, especially those students who have not mastered the skills and strategies necessary for positive academic outcomes. He notes:

> Historically, texts have been central in the literacy development of African American males, with the connections among reading, writing, speaking, and action eminently clear. The literacy development of African American males . . . [has been] connected to larger ideals, such as cultural uplift, economic advancement, resistance to oppression, and intellectual development.[7]

As examples, Tatum cites how abolitionist Frederick Douglass was set on his life's course after reading the political essays and dialogues in *The Columbian Orator*, which Douglass read in his early adolescence, and the documents of abolitionist William Lloyd Garrison. Tatum quotes W. L. Van Deburg's account of the rise and fall of the Black Power movement during the '60s and '70s, when "every brother on a rooftop could quote [anticolonialist Frantz] Fanon."[8] I remember my own early teaching years in the '70s when even those young men who had been deemed illiterate worked their way, collectively and individually, through *The Autobiography of Malcolm X*, offering relevant quotes for any perceived appropriate occasion.

Tatum writes of his success in engaging young African Americans, especially low-income, struggling males, in deep and authentic literacy by choosing appropriate texts. He asserts that "must-read" texts must have four characteristics:

They are intellectually exciting for both students and teachers, they serve as a roadmap and provide apprenticeship, they challenge students cognitively, and they help students apply literacy skills and strategies independently. More specifically, must-read texts should

- engage students in authentic discussions in which they can analyze their realities in the context of the curriculum and discuss strategies for overcoming academic and societal barriers;
- address students' cognitive and affective domains, taking into account students' cultural characteristics;
- connect the social, the economic, and the political to the educational;
- acknowledge that developing skills, increasing test scores, and nurturing students' identities are fundamentally compatible;
- resolve the either-or dilemma of focusing on skill development versus developing intelligence by offering challenges that satisfy both requirements;
- serve as soft role models in the absence of physically present male role models by providing motivation, direction, and hope for the future and suggesting what is worthwhile in life.[9]

It is valuable reading Tatum's books to learn how he has successfully engaged and taught young African American men on whom schools would otherwise have given up. (A list of Tatum's recommended titles for middle and high school students is included in the appendix of the present volume.)

In *Rethinking Mathematics: Teaching Social Justice by the Numbers*, Eric Gutstein and Bob Peterson argue that mathematics should not be taught in a decontextualized, sterile fashion but should be connected to children's culture and experience, be seen as an essential tool for understanding and changing the world, deepen students' understanding of important social matters, connect to other areas of study, and provide an understanding of students' own power as active citizens.

In an example derived from his own teaching, Gutstein and his seventh-grade class undertook a study of racial profiling using mathematics, based on his students' observation that black and Latino drivers were more likely to be stopped by police officers than were white drivers. After reviewing basic probability through hands-on activities, the students became acquainted with several mathematical/scientific concepts: randomness, experiment, simulation, sample size, experimental and theoretical probability, and the law of large numbers (i.e., the more experiments you run, the closer you come to theoretical probabilities.)

They next studied state data based on police reports of racial breakdowns of discretionary traffic stops. Then they compared this data with the ethnic breakdown of the state's population. Groups of students created statistical simulations of the percentages of stops of different ethnic groups by pulling proportionate numbers of differently colored cubes from a cloth bag. The groups then combined their results and analyzed the total simulations as a whole class.

At the end of the unit, students were asked to write about what they had learned, how mathematics had helped them learn it, whether they now believed that racial profiling is a problem, and whatever additional questions the project had brought to mind. The class then discussed the issue and decided whether they should take a next step and publicize their findings.

Mathematics, taught using real-life community problems that clearly affect students' families—and will soon affect students themselves—offers engaging, interesting learning, as well as providing a means for students to feel a part of the school and the mathematics curriculum. Gutstein and Peterson quote Frieda, a ninth-grade student in Chicago who had experienced this kind of mathematics curriculum:

> I thought math was just a subject they implanted on us just because they felt like it, but now I realize that you could use math to defend your rights and realize the injustices around you. . . . I mean, now I think math is truly necessary and I have to admit it, kinda cool. It's sort of like a pass you could use to try to make the world a better place.[10]

As we look to basketball for answers to how to reimagine our schools, one school seems to have gotten a lot of it right. The Urban Prep Academy for Young Men is located in one of the poorest and most dangerous communities in Chicago. Indeed, I was told that some of the young men could not wear their uniforms on the way to school for fear of being attacked, so they carry them in their book bags and change once they get into the building. I visited during Urban Prep's second year of operation, in 2008. Ninety percent of the students received free or reduced-price lunch, and on the opening day of school, the average freshman reads at the sixth-grade level. The school's two administrators were black men, and most of the teachers were young, black, and male, although there were also some white and female teachers.

Every morning, all of the young men, dressed in blazers and ties (help with purchasing these was available where there was a need), assembled in the gym. Instead of standing in homerooms, they were arranged in lines as "prides," like lions. Prides competed in different arenas with each other—highest attendance rate, lowest rate of tardiness, etc.

During this daily gathering, announcements were made of special awards. Although they included sports awards, there was a focus on academics. The morning I was there, one young man was honored for having passed the twelfth-grade state test in tenth grade. Another was honored for having scored in the 20s on the ACT test, although he was only in the ninth grade. But the exceptionally gifted students were not the only ones to receive honors. There were awards for the most-improved student in each class— the Sleeping Giant Awards. There was also an award for the class that had the highest rate for homework completion for the week.

After the announcements, the school began its day with a short speech by one of the students. All students have chances to speak at different functions during the school year. In closing, everyone recited the Urban Prep Creed in unison:

> *We believe.*
> *We are the young men of Urban Prep.*
> *We are college bound.*
> *We are exceptional—not because we say it, but because we work hard at it.*
> *We will not falter in the face of any obstacle placed before us.*
> *We are dedicated, committed and focused.*
> *We never succumb to mediocrity, uncertainty or fear.*
> *We never fail because we never give up.*
> *We make no excuses.*
> *We choose to live honestly, nonviolently and honorably.*
> *We respect ourselves and, in doing so, respect all people.*
> *We have a future for which we are accountable.*
> *We have a responsibility to our families, community and world.*
> *We are our brothers' keepers.*
> *We believe in ourselves.*
> *We believe in each other. We believe in Urban Prep.*
> *WE BELIEVE.*[11]

This creed was prominently displayed in every classroom. During class, teachers made frequent reference to different phrases in the creed, as it might apply to what was happening in the classroom.

In one tenth-grade history class I visited, students were discussing slavery: "house slavery, skilled slavery, urban slavery, and mental slavery." The students sat in a circle and were addressed by the teacher and each other as "Doctor." Here is a snippet of the discussion:

> Student: "I'd like to build on what my fellow colleague stated... (he berates hip hop.)"
> (All through the discussion the teacher refers to hip hop lyrics to challenge the students. He also points to relevant statements in the creed.)
> Student: "Our community just doesn't have the right state of mind."
> Teacher: "Why do you say that, Dr. Johnson?"
> Student: "We don't stick together; we do violence to each other."
> Student: "Hurt people hurt [other] people."
> Student: "I'd like to contradict my colleague: that's an excuse, Dr. Regis."
> Student: "It's not an excuse; it's just the way people are. That's what happens when people get angry."
> Teacher: "What about Frederick Douglass? Frederick Douglass was angry."
> Student: "Frederick Douglass used education to hurt those who hurt him."
> Student: "You can use your mind to hurt your enemies."
> Student: "We just don't have enough role models in the community."
> Teacher: (Goes around the room lightly touching the backs of the young men as he counts aloud.) "We have nineteen men in this room and over three hundred in this school!"

Student: "We have to be the solution we want to see in the community."

The teachers at Urban Prep took seriously the role of teacher/ guide of the young men in their charge. When the young men failed, the teachers looked to themselves and their strategies to find solutions. The Urban Prep Charter Academy's Instructional Theory of Action describes the teachers' beliefs about their work, which includes to:

- provide a culturally relevant curriculum that centralizes, rather than marginalizes, the complete experience of urban young men;
- take responsibility for teaching and engaging our young men in learning, whether they are indifferent, resistant, or achieving significantly below grade level;
- gear our teaching styles, strategies, and techniques to the learning styles of urban young men.[12]

Today the school is still working to improve its instruction, but even though many of the students still do not score as highly as hoped on state tests, a large percentage of graduating seniors have been accepted at four-year colleges. Some will continue to struggle, but they have worked on persistence, embracing challenges, and seeking help when needed. They have been helped to develop the character skills that would allow them to invest time and energy into the necessary practice to excel. Tim King, who founded the academy with a group of African American leaders in education, business, and government, has opened several more campuses and already has over two thousand enrollment applications.

The neighborhoods in which our children grow up often provide the cultural environment that produces the drive to practice and excel in basketball. Our role as educators is to create the cultural environment that will give them the drive also to practice and excel in academics.

Social psychologist Claude Steele has surmised that the most significant issue affecting the lowered achievement of African Americans in school is not their poverty nor their violent neighborhoods nor even their poor prior preparation. His research and observations lead him to believe that the biggest barrier to black students' school achievement is their "disidentification" with school. Because the school holds such negative views about black culture, so many unexamined yet frequently enacted beliefs about black intellectual competence, such a paucity of curricular offerings in which African American students can find themselves represented, the students believe themselves unaccepted by and unacceptable to the school. They, in turn, choose to maintain a sense of self-esteem by disregarding and "disidentifying" with the institutions that think so poorly of them. Steele says that the only offer for acceptance made by schools to black students is this:

> You can be valued and rewarded in school (and society) . . . but you must first master the culture and ways of the American mainstream, and since that mainstream (as it is represented) is essentially white, this means you must give up many particulars of being black—styles of speech and appearance, value priorities, preferences.[13]

Accepting such a bargain could come only with a large serving of self-deprecation, at best. But we have the opportunity to offer another kind of agreement, one in which students can remain psychically intact *and* achieve academically. Alfred Tatum, Eric Gutstein, the Algebra Project, and the Urban Prep Academy all give us models. If we are really serious about educating *all* of our children, we will follow their leads.

PART FOUR
UNIVERSITY AND BEYOND

10

INVISIBILITY, DISIDENTIFICATION, AND NEGOTIATING BLACKNESS ON CAMPUS

I am a man of substance, of flesh and bone. . . . I am invisible, understand, simply because people refuse to see me. . . . They see only my surroundings, themselves, or figments of their imagination.
    —Ralph Ellison, *Invisible Man*, 1953

My daughter's often difficult travels through school have helped me understand my own journeys, as well as those of other African American children. As I have perceived her changing needs over the years, she has alternated between predominantly white and predominantly black school settings. Each setting has had its own advantages and disadvantages. After searching for the perfect preschool—one that had a good curriculum, one that was not too far from home, etc., I located one that accepted my precocious almost-three-year-old into its predominantly white student body. There were lovely play corners, exciting manipulatives, and lots of music and art. Yet, my child, previously potty trained, began having accidents. The teachers tried all sorts of strategies—reminding her to go to the bathroom, allowing her to get up from nap time, giving her rewards for dry days—but nothing seemed to work. One day when I picked her up, I asked in exasperation, "Maya, what is going on? Why are you wetting your pants all the time?" She answered without taking her eyes off the toy she was playing with, "Maybe because I'm invisible." That comment sent me reeling into my own remembered feelings of invisibility when desegregation landed me into a newly integrated but still predominantly white school in ninth grade. There, the newly arrived black students never seemed to be acknowledged in any positive way in classrooms, in the choir, the art room, or on athletic playing fields. I wasn't sure what was going on with Maya, but when I transferred her to a smaller, family-based, African American setting, the problem disappeared. Along with her claims of invisibility.

Many years later, Maya expressed dismay at how she felt at a predominantly white high school. "No one hears me. I say something and they act like I'm not even there." I initially thought that, like many teenagers, she was just lodging complaints about having to go to school at all. But then, when I spoke to one of her teachers, he told me that Maya was not really engaged with school. He added that the eleventh graders were supposed to attend at least one faculty meeting and participate in the discussion and that Maya had not done so. When I confronted her with the complaint, she said, "Mom, I *did* go! I actually went to two meetings, and I did try to participate, but nobody responded." Invisible again.

In a society that has alternately ignored their existence or challenged their presence, African Americans have in many instances had to cope with a sense of not being seen. Bill is forty-seven years old, a Yale graduate, and African American. As a part of his management position in a large corporation, he frequently takes clients to lunch or dinner. One evening he took a white client to an exclusive restaurant in New York. As the two approached the desk, the maitre d' completely ignored Bill and asked the guest if they had a reservation. After dinner, the waiter returned Bill's credit card to his guest. Out on the street, the client immediately got a cab, while Bill tried unsuccessfully for fifteen minutes. When yet another cab ignored Bill and stopped for a white couple, Bill exploded. Invisible.

Anderson J. Franklin, professor at Lynch School of Education at Boston College, coined a phrase for it: "invisibility syndrome"— black men and women faced with disillusionment when talents, potential, and basic humanity are ignored, misrepresented, or misguided.[1]

Time after time, black students in predominantly white institutions tell of making a statement in class and not having the comment acknowledged until a white student repeats their point. (One student I interviewed called it the Elvis Presley syndrome—"white people wouldn't acknowledge or appreciate black music until Elvis Presley stole it.")

Invisibility is not the only problem. There are times when African Americans find themselves hypervisible, especially when more than one dares to congregate in one place. No matter the setting, there is often a sense that others are watching warily, that they expect some sudden assault on their well-being: two black professors take an elevator in a hotel to their rooms, only to see, as the elevator stops on other floors, that several white women decide not to get on. A few years ago the Black Student Union at Harvard organized a spring dodgeball game on Harvard's quad. The police showed up almost as soon as the game started—a result of several concerned calls that "outsiders" were invading the campus. Invisibility inside the classroom, hypervisibility outside the classroom.

The reality of African Americans in this country leaves little doubt that, historically, black people have been devalued and stigmatized. Doubts arise, however, when the argument is made that devaluation and stigmatization—even with a black president—are still a fundamental aspect of current-day America. The paramount proof of that argument is the still-unfolding tragedy of post-Katrina New Orleans. In 2005, many of us watched in horror as people on rooftops and at the Superdome pleaded with the world for help. We saw elderly mothers and tiny babies dying of dehydration or lack of necessary medical attention. We saw whole neighborhoods ravaged by rising water. But there was much we did not see, much that we were not allowed to see. The entire grisly story, the story of how poor and darker-skinned citizens were not just victims of the storm but victims of intentional governmental policy, may never reach the consciousness of the larger American public.

Lance Hill, with whom I have worked on issues of education and equity, is a white researcher affiliated with Tulane University and a longtime resident of New Orleans. He and his wife did not evacuate during Katrina. He wrote a report of his experiences with an intentional blockade in the days following the disaster:

> On Friday, September 2nd, my wife and I packed up my car with all the supplies we could gather and I began the first of four runs in to the convention center, where I encountered no danger; only grateful and orderly people desperate for food and water. On my fourth run I was met by a contingent of New Orleans and State Police who ordered me not to distribute the water I had brought. A line of white state policemen with automatic weapons faced off against the crowd who were shouting to let me unload my supplies. It was an explosive situation and the police quickly relented but told me not to return.
>
> There was never any question in my mind that these officers were acting on orders to prevent relief from getting to flood vic-

tims. My wife and I remained in New Orleans for more than a month during martial law, for the most part taking care of elderly people in the unflooded areas, and every law enforcement officer and soldier that we met told us the same thing: they had been ordered not to provide citizens with food, water, or medical aid.

Red Cross officials are on record [as] saying they had relief supplies in New Orleans but were ordered not to distribute them. American Red Cross president Marsha "Marty" Evans went on national television and said that the Louisiana Department of Homeland Security (LA-DHS) had ordered the Red Cross not to provide relief supplies to refugees inside the city, arguing that the presence of the Red Cross "would keep people from evacuating and encourage others to come to the city. . . . The Red Cross web site carried a FAQ repeating that authorities had prevented them from providing relief supplies to the storm victims at the Convention Center.[2]

Of course, those at the Superdome and Convention Center had no way to evacuate, as promised buses took days to materialize. Other reasons given as to why no aid was forthcoming to those stranded in the Convention Center was that it was too dangerous for even the police to enter. However, the *Washington Post* published a news story reporting that one day after the relief blockade order was issued, a twelve-member New Orleans SWAT team led by Sgt. Hans Ganthier, entered the convention center to transport out two white women, the wife of a Jefferson Parish sheriff's deputy, who had requested rescue, and her friend. Hill adds, "The police literally had to make their way past dying elderly blacks in order to extricate the two white women. That incident alone should answer the question of whether there was a double standard based on color for who deserved official protection and aid at the center."[3]

Many other firsthand stories exist that will likely never be published, that painfully illustrate just how marginalized poor black people became during the crisis. The African American population still has not recovered—suffering both from the effects of the storm itself and also from the treatment they received at the hands of those in power. Only a few days after the storm, a white Louisiana legislator, Representative Richard Baker, was overheard making a comment to a lobbyist about the government housing inhabited mostly by African Americans: "We couldn't [clean up public housing], but God did."[4] And, indeed, even though there were analyses done by MIT engineers saying the public housing buildings were sound, the government chose to demolish them, displacing hundreds of black families. Six years later, policies are still in place making it difficult for African Americans to return to New Orleans. The children I see in schools are clearly suffering from untreated post-traumatic stress disorder, and any counselor today at schools housing New Orleans children will report that violence, depression, drug use, and suicides are rampant—much more evident than pre-Katrina. This is also the case for untreated adults. Even for those who appear to function relatively normally, there is a phrase often used today, six years later, by New Orleans natives when they are forgetful; experience extreme mood swings; or have trouble concentrating, sleeping, or solving a problem: "It's my Katrina mind." I began to understand some of the deep-seated feelings when I was asked in 2009 by a Katrina survivor, "How are you supposed to go on when you realize your own country was ready to let you die?"

I address just a fragment of the Katrina story here to make the point that we are far from a color-blind society, that African Americans are still devalued, stigmatized, and made invisible. Even African Americans who never resided in New Orleans have the television images of desperate black men, women, and children seared into their memories as a perpetual reminder of our government's response to black suffering. My friend who works as an engineer in Africa told me that his Nigerian colleagues were mesmerized by the images transmitted on their televisions and asked my friend more than once, "Are you sure New Orleans is in America?" Katrina is a "big story," but there are many, many smaller ones. These represent a delicate, troublesome facet of the unhealed parts of American race relations.

Although I seldom meet an overt, conscious racist in the circles I travel, I frequently encounter unconscious, subtle racism that remains unaddressed—or if it is addressed by those who are its victims, they are labeled as "oversensitive" or "too thin-skinned." I may have first encountered the phenomenon when, as a new college student, I had just traveled the long road from the overt racism of Louisiana desegregation to the staunchly liberal, left-wing Antioch College in Ohio. I was exhilarated, not only with being on my own for the first time, but with the newly discovered politics of liberation. I had never before met white people who so openly voiced radical perspectives. I was not prepared, however, for the more subtle aspects of racial stereotyping. One still-vivid example is when one of my professors asked me about my educational background. I explained to him that I grew up in an all-black neighborhood, had gone to segregated all-black schools, with all-black teachers until my last years in high school. With a smile of what I am sure he thought was encouragement, he asked, "How in the world did you ever learn how to write?" He had no clue that he had insulted my community, my family, and my teachers.

Such insults occur daily. It is hard to describe the feeling of being unvalued in one's own country. I recall when African American ice skater Debi Thomas represented the United States in the Winter Olympics. Although Debi was our best chance to win a gold medal, all the attention in the United States was focused on a young white German skater, Katerina Witt. What must Debi have thought after all her hard work, about her country's focusing its attention on her competitor, frequently referred to by the U.S. commentators as a beautiful "ice princess." Serena and Venus Williams must feel similarly when sportscasters lavish attention on their young white opponents during their tennis matches.

So many young girls have been made to feel "unpretty" when their efforts to be princesses were dashed by classmates' acceptance of Disney's portrayal of what a princess "really" looks like—"You can't be a princess. Princesses are white!" For so long, aspiring princesses could only compare themselves to Snow White, Cinderella, or Sleeping Beauty. Then finally in the name of diversity there was the Chinese Mulan, the Middle Eastern Jasmine, and even the little mermaid Ariel. But still no model of a princess for little African American girls. Finally, after decades of complaints, the company finally created Princess Tiana in 2009, who, however, I was told by my own young great niece, spent most of the movie as a frog.

But the damage has already been done, and not solely by Disney. One of my graduate students, Kami Henley, took on the project of repeating the "doll study" made famous by the Clarks in the fight for desegregation.[5] In the latter study, researchers Mamie and Kenneth Clark showed two dolls, different only in color, to young black children and asked them a number of questions. A majority of the children answered that they thought the white doll was nicer, prettier, and better to play with. They identified the black doll as bad, ugly, and not as good to play with. It was particularly wrenching when some of these young children, asked which doll looked like them, hesitantly chose the black doll, which they had already labeled with negative attributes. A young black teenager, Kiri Davis, replicated the study with a group of black preschoolers in Harlem and got almost identical results in 2006. My student, Kami Henley, again replicated the study in Louisiana in 2011, and found the same results, with the percentages of children attributing positive features to the white doll even remaining the same as the original assessment in the

1940s and '50s. As painful as it is to admit as a mother, aunt, and teacher of black children, clearly our young people still internalize the message that their society devalues and negatively stereotypes them.

A sad but comically ironic example of the place of African Americans in this society is a story in Patricia Williams's book *Seeing a Color Blind Future*. In this book, Williams challenges the notion that we have achieved a color-blind society and wonders if we will ever get there. She describes her attempt to get a mortgage to buy a house in an all-white community. As a result of her discussions with her lender, she realized that by purchasing her house she would be devaluing her investment by bringing down her own property value.[6]

These examples are certainly not life and death. Some seem absolutely trivial. And, in isolation, they are. In the late '70s, however, Harvard researcher Chester Pierce coined the term "microaggressions," which were identified as small psychic insults, any one of which would not be of great consequence but when added together over time create a deadly psychological assault. Pierce equated sustaining microaggressions to ingesting minuscule amounts of arsenic over a protracted time. No one dose would cause harm, but over time the consequence would be death.[7]

The common currently cited definition of microaggression is put forth by Columbia University psychologist Derald Wing Sue and colleagues: "Brief and commonplace daily verbal, behavioral, or environmental indignities, whether intentional or unintentional, that communicate hostile, derogatory, or negative racial slights and insults toward people of color."

Sue et al. also studied the consequences of enduring microaggressions. They found that people felt demeaned by implied messages, such as "you do not belong," "you are abnormal," "you are intellectually inferior," "you cannot be trusted," and "you are all the same."[8] Those on the receiving end of microaggressions also reported feeling powerlessness, invisibility, pressure to comply, loss of integrity, and pressure to represent one's group.

And this brings us to a discussion of black students on college campuses. The completion rate of black students in college is approximately 45 percent, which, according to the *Journal of Blacks in Higher Education* is about 20 percentage points lower than the rate for whites.[9] The most common reasons given for this dropout disparity are poor preparation, financial issues, lack of resources, job ceilings, poor schools, and poverty-influenced family issues.

But psychologist and researcher Claude Steele suggests that there may be other reasons for the disparity. His argument is based on several sets of statistics. He relates that racial differences in retention rates exist even at high-income levels, with students with high-preparation levels. He notes that scores don't seem to make much of a difference in college dropout rates, regardless of race. Those with 800 combined scores on the SAT are no more likely to flunk out than those with combined scores of 1200–1500. But race makes a difference: where 2–11 percent of whites flunk out, 18–33 percent of blacks flunk out, even at the highest SAT level.[10]

Further, given any level of school preparation (as measured by both tests and earlier grades), blacks somehow achieve less in subsequent schooling than whites—they have poorer grades and lower graduation rates and take longer to graduate—no matter how strong their preparation is. Put another way, when Steele and his colleagues looked at one highly rated college, attaining the *same* achievement level required better preparation for blacks than for whites. Among students with a C+ average, the mean ACT score for blacks was at the ninety-eighth percentile; for whites, the thirty-fourth percentile.

So what is going on with black underachievement and dropping out at the college level? With our current economy I would not at all rule out financial concerns, but since many of these concerns affect middle-class whites as much as middle-class blacks, I am further suggesting that some of the culpability may lie in the same factors that plague African Americans in our general society: invisibility, devaluing, stigma, and stereotyping, often taking the form of unconscious racially based microaggressions.

This contention is supported by research conducted over many years. In a 2000 study that looked at the perceptions of 538 students enrolled at white universities, Julie Ancis et al. found that

> African Americans consistently reported more negative experiences compared with Asian Americans, Latino/a and white students. Specifically, African American students experienced greater racial-ethnic hostility; greater pressure to conform to stereotypes; less equitable treatment by faculty, staff, and teaching assistants; and more faculty racism than did other groups.[11]

These findings are consistent with many previous studies showing that even after desegregation had been in place for over twenty years in most institutions, African American students still found white campuses psychologically and culturally hostile.[12]

As Beverly Tatum says in *"Why Are All the Black Kids Sitting Together in the Cafeteria?"*

> Whether it is the loneliness of being routinely overlooked as a lab partner in science courses, the irritation of being continually asked by curious classmates about Black hairstyles, the discomfort of being singled out by a professor to give the "Black perspective" in class discussion, the pain of racist graffiti scrawled on dormitory room doors, the insult of racist jokes circulated through campus e-mail, or the injury inflicted by racial epithets (and sometimes beer bottles) hurled from a passing car, Black students on predominantly White college campus must cope with ongoing affronts to their racial identity.[13]

When I speak to students on today's campuses, they refer to much of what I have previously discussed—they say something in class, but they are not "heard" by the class until a white student repeats their comment with no reference to their prior comment; they constantly have a feeling of being in the wrong place; they feel that they are viewed as part of a group and not as individuals. They say that whenever black issues are discussed the class and the professor look to them to state what black people want, think, or do. One commented that he felt like saying, "Gee, I missed the meeting so it's not my turn to be the spokesman. Check with me next week."

They also take umbrage with the assumption that black students are present through some kind of affirmative action program and that they need academic assistance. One young woman told me of waiting outside a professor's office to get a signature on a class form. When the professor came out of his office and saw a white student and a black student sitting in the waiting area, he assumed that it was the black student who had come to get academic tutoring.

Another student told me that she couldn't shake the feeling that no one really knew who she was or cared about what she really wanted. She felt she was seen either as a member of a group who was there to "save the college" by increasing diversity, or she was there to be a part of the college's missionary-like efforts to "save black people."

Steele suggests that these feelings that black students carry with them start a process of what he calls "disidentification" with school. He relays the story of a young woman he was asked to mentor when he took a position at a university. This young woman had planned to become a doctor but was now planning to drop out. Steele follows her steps after she arrives on campus:

> Her recruitment and admission stress her minority status perhaps
> more strongly than it has been stressed at any other time in her

life. She is offered academic and social support services, further implying that she is "at risk" (even though, contrary to common belief, the vast majority of black college students are admitted with qualifications well above the threshold for whites). Once on campus, she enters a socially circumscribed world in which blacks—still largely separate from whites—have lower status; this is reinforced by a sidelining of minority material and interests in the curriculum and in university life. And she can sense that everywhere in this new world her skin color places her under suspicion of intellectual inferiority. All of this gives her the double vulnerability I spoke of: she risks confirming a particular incompetence, at chemistry or a foreign language, for example; but she also risks confirming the racial inferiority she is suspected of—a judgment that can feel as close at hand as a mispronounced word or an ungrammatical sentence. In reaction, usually to some modest setbacks, she withdraws, hiding her troubles from instructors, counselors, even other students. Quickly, I believe, a psychic defense takes over. She disidentifies with achievement; she changes her self-conception, her outlook and values, so that achievement is no longer important to her self-esteem. She may continue to feel pressure to stay in school—from her parents, even from the potential advantages of a college degree. But now she is psychologically insulated from her academic life, like a disinterested visitor. Cool, unperturbed. But, like a painkilling drug, disidentification undoes her future as it relieves her vulnerability.[14]

Psychologist Jacqueline Fleming in her 1984 groundbreaking book *Blacks in College: A Comparative Study of Students' Success in Black and in White Institutions* summarized the research to that point, which also reflects research conducted since that date: "The fact that black students must matriculate in an atmosphere that feels hostile arouses defensive reactions that interfere with intellectual performance. . . . They display academic demotivation and think less of their abilities. They profess losses of energy."[15]

Psychologists Richard Nisbett and Andrew Reaves joined Steele to study black college-student achievement and found that attitudes related to disidentification were more strongly predictive of grades than any measure of academic preparation. Disidentification reduces performance across the board.

What else contributes to disidentification with school? One factor is the suggestion that the way you act is wrong, that you must give up identifiably African American cultural norms in order to succeed. Another element is the curriculum. Typical university curricula leave out the contributions of people of color to American culture, except in special courses in African American Studies, thus marginalizing both the students and the information. A third element contributing to disidentification is the identification of remedial and special programs with African Americans. This almost ensures that black faces will be linked to academic problems.

Steele and colleague Lisa Brown looked at black students' grades in the 1950s and the 1980s. They focused the study only on those with above-average entry credentials. They found that while African Americans' grades in the 1950s improved the longer they were in college, those who graduated in the 1980s had worsening grades the longer they were in college.[16] Black students on today's campuses may experience less overt prejudice than did their 1950s counterparts but, ironically, may be more racially vulnerable. Steele elaborates on the environment the students of the '80s experienced. "A remedial orientation put their abilities under suspicion, deflected their ambitions, distanced them from their successes and painted them with their failures."[17] In many of today's colleges, these conditions remain unchanged. It is perhaps easier to fortify oneself against blatant bias than against the constant onslaught of the underground microaggressions of modern racial relations.

To summarize, when humans feel they are devalued, stigmatized, or made invisible in a setting, they either protest or withdraw. Protest is a more hopeful sign, as the protesters view at least the possibility of change. Withdrawers disidentify with the institution, define themselves as not a part of the setting, and seek to value themselves outside its parameters. Disidentified students become aliens in the academic world.

So what is the solution? Of course the first thing we must do is to strive to find the funds to make being a student possible. As federal and state programs are cut, those who are least able to afford a college education are most at risk. Many low-income students have to work so many hours that they may find themselves flunking out or having to drop out. We may not have much control over funding, but our collective voices may influence some of the powers-that-be to invest in our country's future by supporting college educations for all citizens.

Although thoughtful and wise educators will come up with many more, I will suggest here four courses of action to support African American students that are much more in the control of college faculty and administrators. These actions, if adopted, will reduce the risk that students will become disidentified with their higher educational institutions. Much of my understanding comes from the education of students in K–12, but the more I work with young (and old) college students of color, the more I realize the similarities. Students of all ages need to feel welcome.

The first element of welcoming, I believe, is to value students of color. If what is meaningful and important to a teacher is to become meaningful and important to a student, the student must feel valued by teachers for his or her potential as a *person*—not as a representative of the race, not as a means to university diversity, not as a weakness to be strengthened. How much do university faculty members know about their students? What kinds of relationships have been forged outside of classrooms? What do we know about students' dreams and struggles?

The power of valuing a student was brought home to me when I took Maya around to visit a number of colleges. Having read a lot about different institutions, I was taken with Loren Pope's idea of "colleges that change lives."[18] I escorted my eighteen-year-old to several of these wonderful institutions, where smiling, professional enrollment officers ushered her into their offices to discuss her academic interests and what she might want to do at their institution. But the game was over when we visited historically black Florida A&M (FAMU) in Tallahassee. When we arrived at the first office, the enrollment director rose from her chair, came around the desk and enveloped Maya in a huge hug, saying, "I'm so glad to see you, Baby! Welcome to your new home; you're going to be our next baby rattler [the school mascot is the rattlesnake] and we can't wait for you to get here. Now come here and let me tell you what you have to do next." The previous schools were quickly forgotten, and Maya did not want to look at any others. She had been welcomed "home."

Although predominantly white schools may not be able to provide the cultural welcome that FAMU did, once students are on their campuses they can make sure that someone asks the students on a regular basis how comfortable they feel in classrooms, if they have adjusted to the college setting, or what could make their experience better. We have to be willing to allow ourselves to be critiqued if we are to ensure that individual students of color feel that they are valuable additions to the college campus.

A second proposal to increase student identification within the university setting is to avoid remedial programs and push for challenging curricula—*with support*. Racially identifiable remediation programs only serve to make African American students—and their professors and other students—question their intellectual worth.

A classic example of challenge with support can be found in the work of Philip Uri Treisman. Treisman's black students at the University of California in the late 1970s performed at the bottom of his mathematics classes. In response, Treisman developed the Mathematics Workshop Program, where students were recruited into study groups to collectively tackle difficult calculus concepts. The workshop was referred to as an "honors workshop," and provided difficult problems, often beyond the scope of the actual course in which the students were enrolled. Thus, students were not labeled as remedial but as advanced. Even students with limited preparation (math SAT scores in the 300s) excelled when they realized that no one knew everything and that working together could provide the understanding they needed.[19] The success of this model has continued into the 2000s,[20] with universities around the country replicating its effectiveness.

Steele commented about the program, "The wisdom of these tactics is their subtext message: 'You are valued in this program because of your academic potential—regardless of your current skill level. You have no more to fear than the next person, and since the work is difficult, success is a credit to your ability, and a setback is a reflection only of the challenge.'"[21] Remediation crushes; challenge fortifies. Where students are valued and challenged, they are likely to succeed.

Educator Michele Foster studied a teacher at a community college in Massachusetts for keys to her exceptional success with her low-income students of color. One of the students interviewed in the research commented:

> When I first walked into her class, my impression was that she was very stern and that you were gonna have to work yourself to death to get a good mark. I remember she said, "You are going to learn

this Management information or die trying." But what sets her apart from the other instructors is that she's more concerned, and that makes you want to work because if not, you feel like you let her down. My problem, which I must get over, is I'm shy in speaking in front of people. She's trying to help me by calling on me. Other instructors know I'm shy and they don't make me answer. She does more; she pushes me to be better and smarter. I didn't know I could be so smart. She makes you feel proud by pointing out the fact that you did get it right. She doesn't make you feel stupid if you don't know. She'll say, "I'm disappointed in you," instead of "you're stupid." She can embarrass you, but she doesn't degrade you.[22]

Before I discuss my third suggestion, I feel I should reiterate that points one and two are inseparable. You cannot value students as intellectual beings without being willing to challenge them, and if they don't feel valued, they will resist being challenged.

The third aspect of creating a welcoming environment for African American students on college campuses is to ensure that their complaints about racism are not minimized. Even if the insult seems minimal or "explainable," understand that microaggressions occur in these students' lives on a constant basis. It is actually a good sign that they are willing to complain and have not given up the belief that they will ever be heard. The thing to keep in mind is that subtle doses of allegorical arsenic eat away at the soul. Address the arsenic, no matter how small the dose seems. We must be willing to listen, to accept their perspective, and to attempt change if necessary.

My final suggestion involves the inclusion of African American culture. While it is important to create a social environment that is hospitable to all cultures, I focus this conversation on what happens in academics. There are three areas of classroom life that are amenable to cultural adaptation: curriculum, pedagogy, and interactional patterns.

Black people and black culture have historically been intricately involved in creating the larger American culture. Indeed, the United States of America would not exist were it not for the labor of enslaved Africans. Further, American music, food, literature, art, and many inventions that make our life what it is all bear the stamp of the children of Africa. Our very democracy would not have been forged without the black-led moral battle waged in the country's struggle with granting civil rights to all Americans. Yet most of our college classes virtually ignore the larger culture's debt to its darker citizens. There is no course in the college curriculum that should not include the contributions and perspectives of African Americans. I have become so inured to the paucity of knowledge of African American contributions that every year I am shocked but not surprised to realize that not only are our K–12 students of all colors virtually ignorant about all things black (with the exception of Rosa Parks and Martin Luther King, with which they are bombarded every February for twelve years), but their teachers are equally ignorant. So many young teachers know little of even the Civil Rights Movement. And they are ignorant because their college classes taught them nothing. Except in special, marginalized electives, everything black-influenced has barely peripheral status in college classrooms. And when one cannot see oneself anywhere represented in what is deemed important to learn, how can identification with the learning occur?

Another aspect of culturally influenced academics has to do with how we teach. One consistent but often ignored aspect of African American learning styles has to do with whether teaching begins with the big picture and works down to the details, or whether it begins with subskills and works up to the global. Traditional teaching favors the latter—first you learn the pieces, then you put them together for the whole. African Americans tend toward the former. Students often want the big ideas, the big story, first. They want the "back story" of whatever is being studied—who created it? Why? What is it used for? What other perspectives exist? What controversies surround it? They also want to know how it is connected to real life, how the knowledge might be useful. Can what is being studied help their community in some way? Will they be given an opportunity to use the information in some real task? For many African American students, it is important to actually "do" scholarship, not just study it. By engaging in the doing—conducting research, presenting findings, publishing writings—no matter how limited or amateur the end-product, they will be more willing to do the work to refine the component parts. By participating in the "doing," they are also joining the "academic club." They come to feel that they have membership in a guild of scholars and thus become more identified with the university.

Culturally sensitive classroom life should also include collaboration and group interaction in the name of academic achievement. Many African American students have gotten to college by spending many years of earlier schooling individually focused on their studies. They may have been influenced by their parents to keep a low social profile and stay away from others who might divert their attention from school achievement. This behavior runs contrary to the norms of African American culture and is actually detrimental to high achievement in difficult university classes. Treisman's work in mathematics exemplifies the need to help African American students work collaboratively to achieve academic success.

Students report that a classroom culture of cooperation and collaboration also makes it easier to engage because they feel more secure and less vulnerable. One of the students in the class Michele Foster studied put it this way:

> In some classes you are afraid to raise your hand. In Ms. Morris' class people aren't afraid because Ms. Morris says "help them out." In Ms. Barnes' class you feel like you're swimming alone and if

she doesn't help you out you'll drown. In Ms. Morris' class you
know if you jump into the water, someone will come by and help
you out; you won't drown. I'm afraid to even ask questions in Ms.
Barnes' class.[23]

The ideal is to seek to build a social connection around academics. Ms. Morris and Treisman did it within a specific course. One
black fraternity did it by making academic focus an element of
membership. Iota Phi Theta at San Jose State is credited with increasing the graduation rate of its members to an astounding 90
percent—almost triple the 30 percent rate of the school's overall
African American population. Frat brothers say they bond during "step shows" (percussive dance routines) that travel to other
schools for competitions. But on the way home, they pull out their
books and study. Like Treisman's and Ms. Morris's students, they
created a sense of social bonding around academic achievement.[24]

These are but a few suggestions for an undoubtedly complex
problem. There is no simple recipe, and the only real solution is for
humans who care about bettering the university campus—indeed
opening the country to new possibilities—to confer, collaborate,
argue, ponder, and act to fashion a space for real dialogue and
understanding.

The path to healing racial relations in our society is not an easy
one. We take a few steps forward, become frightened, it seems, with
new possibilities, and then retreat. Lyrics of the Black National
Anthem not only chronicle the struggles of African Americans
but also the struggle of America to break free of racial divisions:
"Stony the road we trod," as we seek to find the courage and fortitude to create healing.

The ideas shared in this chapter come not from theorizing but
from the "front." Most of my career has been spent in predominantly white institutions of higher learning, where I have been one
of the few black professors to whom students of color—African

American, Latino, Native American—could come to bare their souls, to cry, to shout, to find the fortitude to continue another day. I have listened, consoled, fussed, encouraged, and shared my own experiences in similar situations.

Now I am one of many black professors at a historically black university. My job is still to help dress the wounds inflicted by racism on young black minds, but I have another job as well: to help my white students understand and negotiate issues of race on a predominantly black campus. Many of them are facing these issues for the first time in their lives. I was heartened to receive a letter from a white graduate student, Jodi Lemoine, which she sent at the end of a recent course:

> This class has truly been a "journey" for me on a personal level as well. You came to class the first day and made it okay for me, a white girl, to disagree, share my viewpoint, and ask questions—even hard ones. I have never had a door opened for me like that before. I struggle to put in words what an impact just making it okay for me to participate in a conversation about race at a historically black college had on me. And I think what you will be most pleased to learn is that you have inspired me to provide that classroom environment for the black children who will come to my classroom, and hopefully that kind of environment will exist in the school I will lead one day as an administrator. We have probably said a hundred times this semester that race is the "800 pound elephant in the room." I would never even broach the subject with co-workers, administrators, and certainly never the kids or their parents before this class. What a silly stance to take on an issue that is at the heart of so many challenges in our schools, and so many of these challenges would go away if we would communicate and understand where everyone is coming from, or at least try to.

Although I have centered this chapter on creating an environment in which African American students can be made to feel welcome and gain a sense of identification with the university setting, the benefits are not only for black students. If we can bring all of our students into a space that honors them and engages them by addressing the racially divisive issues that have plagued our country for centuries, if we can "unsilence the dialogue" that barricades our understanding, then I believe the university can be the catalyst to heal this gaping but too often unacknowledged wound in the center of our collective American psyche.

11

WILL IT HELP THE SHEEP?
UNIVERSITY, COMMUNITY, AND PURPOSE

Anthropologists Sol Worth and John Adair tell a story about attempting to conduct a research project on a Navajo reservation. To investigate cultural "frames," they wished to study how films made by Navajo people might differ from those made by individuals socialized in "mainstream" culture.[1]

As good anthropologists, in order to move ahead with the work, they sought to get the permission of the tribal elders. The researchers set out to see an elderly Navajo medicine man, Sam Yazzie. Although the researchers only presented an outline of the conversation, this is my picture of what happened:

A dust-covered pickup truck makes its way down the long, unpaved, perfectly flat road and stops in front of a hogan. Two young white men, dressed in jeans and a little worse for wear, get out of the truck and greet the old man who has come to the door. They've spent time on the reservation, so they know the proper etiquette. They enter the hogan and the three sit at the table. Only after pleasantries have been exchanged and hot tea has been sipped during long periods of amiable silence do the visitors lay out their plan.

The old man sits quietly as they explain their project with the excitement of researchers who've hit upon a novel idea. After they stop talking, the old man is silent for many minutes. Finally, he asks slowly about their proposed research: "Will it hurt the sheep?"

"Oh no!" one of the younger men responds quickly. And both proceed to explain that filming can in no way damage anyone or anything.

The old man sits quietly again with his eyes closed. Finally, after many more minutes, he speaks again: "Will it do them any good?"

This time the researchers are quiet. They glance at each other nervously and finally one says haltingly, "Well, no, not really."

The old man opens his eyes and looking directly at the two younger men says, "Then why do it?"

Why do it? As I think back on my university career to date, I have been trying to identify what I have learned that has assisted me in my quest to keep trying to help the sheep. There are three major lessons that have guided my personal path.

Be Courageous

Education is not a job for the weak-willed. There are so many elements that fight against us—senseless bureaucracies, unfeeling systems, societal inequities, to name but a few. It is not easy to keep one's courage up. One of my primary role models for courage has been Dr. Robert P. Moses. Bob Moses is a hero in the history of America. Many books and films have chronicled his journey in the Civil Rights Movement. As a young man in his early twenties, he left his job as a math teacher in New York and traveled to Mississippi, where he came to be one of the primary leaders of the Mississippi Civil Rights Movement. Bob, and the young Freedom Fighters who came to view him as their leader, faced beatings, imprisonment, and even death to bring the vote to the black sharecroppers of the South and democracy to America.

Today, Bob leads a new Civil Rights Movement—Quality Education as a Civil Right. Through the National Algebra Project, which he founded, Bob seeks to provide quality education in mathematics to the young people who have been failed by the education system, who have up to this time been given what he refers to as a sharecropper education—an education fit for those who are least valued in our society. In this new role he still exudes courage, speaking truth to power—from school system administrators to the U.S. Congress—and pushing school systems to turn their attention to the children many do not want to see.

The Algebra Project is designed not only to ensure that the most disadvantaged students in our country have the opportunity to learn higher-order mathematics but also to learn how to advocate for their educational rights. Bob asserts that in our present society, learning mathematics is crucial to achieving full educational citizenship. Students who do not advance in mathematics are predestined by middle school to be excluded from the possibility of attending college. And education *is* the new civil rights agenda.

As a part of his Algebra Project, Bob worked with a group of students in Mississippi who initially scored in the lowest quartile of a low-performing school. These young people were representatives of the "throwaway" class from whom school systems expect little. After much negotiation with the school district, Bob became their regular mathematics teacher for four years, from ninth through twelfth grades. Under his and other committed teachers' tutelage, all but one member of that "low-performing" class entered college.

Bob subsequently worked with a class of students from a high school in Miami, again students identified in the lowest quartile of the lowest-performing school. These students were primarily of Haitian origin; many were new immigrants, most with parents who did not speak English. No one in the larger society has had many expectations for these young people. As a part of Bob's work, he insisted that the students not only learn mathematics but have the opportunity to be exposed to many advanced topics. A part of his plan was to organize a summer institute for these young people and some additional students from other low-performing high schools. The program, organized through the Center for Urban Education and Innovation, which I directed at the time, allowed the Haitian American, African American, and Hispanic American students to stay on our campus at Florida International University for the six-week program. The young people spent ten-hour days working with Bob and other instructors in mathematics, language arts, linguistics, sociology, and the creative arts. Students from the Mississippi program, now young college students, came to Miami as counselors for their younger peers.

Although the adults in charge were run ragged by the end of the six weeks—keeping up with forty fifteen-year-olds for twenty-four hours a day is no easy task—the young people begged to stay longer. Despite their earlier homesickness and initial status as low performers, they were excited about learning new things, and all indicated that they, as one young man declared, learned more in six weeks than they had in nine years of school. The specific topics they tackled were impressive: language variation in the African diaspora, the geometry of art, ethnography, critical race theory, filmmaking, and computer programming.

At age seventy-four, Bob went in every day to teach math. He had the same challenges as most teachers. I remember on the first day, when the students didn't know the adults, and certainly didn't know Bob, they talked and played during the presentations about the program by the other adults. When it was Bob's turn to speak, he stood in front of the twenty-five teenagers without saying a word. Silently, he stood there for at least ten minutes. As he stood, the young people eventually became silent and looked at him. One could have heard a pin drop when Bob finally said, quietly, "I don't expect you ever to talk while we are trying to tell you something again. The people here care about you, and you need to listen to them." He went on quietly to present the program to them. I can't say that the kids never talked again while we were trying to teach, but they never interrupted Bob! That took courage to stand quietly in front of twenty-five antsy teenagers!

Those young people have recently graduated from high school. They are amazingly articulate. They have grown physically, emotionally, and intellectually. They are working, through the Young People's Project, to tutor elementary school children in math. Recently, Tommy, who in 2010 was arrested at a protest for better schools, and Cherlynn, whom we thought we might lose when she became pregnant in tenth grade but who came back a week after having the baby and brought the baby to closing ceremonies, spoke at a research conference to adults. They talked eloquently about how the children they tutor don't believe in themselves and how they are victims of high-stakes testing. They said that they are doing for these elementary schoolchildren what they had hoped would have been done for them when they were younger. They spoke with reverence about Bob Moses and said that he believed in them and taught them to believe in themselves. They said he wouldn't give up on them, so they won't give up on the younger kids, even when they find themselves frustrated trying to teach them.

It is Bob's courage that has kept the program going. Many times the principal or the school district or the university wanted to close it down. Without ever raising his voice, Bob Moses brought the power of his belief in the children and their potential to the systems that affect their lives, and to the children themselves.

Like Bob Moses, we teachers must take up the cause of those children who are so often dismissed by the system. That means never giving up on them; refusing to accept failure; being their advocates and pushing them and the systems that block their success. It also means having the courage to find like-minded people—on faculties, in the community, wherever they may be—and joining together to do this difficult work. One person cannot change the world alone. We all have to step out of our personal comfort zones to create courageous, united efforts.

Learn Humility

I have come away from years of spending time in cultures and communities other than my own with a deep belief that people are experts on their own lives. While we in academia are predisposed to accept unquestioningly research studies written by others about marginalized groups, these studies must be read skeptically. No one is an expert on someone else's life. Research can lead educators to questions they may ask their students or their students' parents. It can lead them to deeper observations in different kinds of situations. But nothing can replace listening to what people have to say about themselves. I have learned that I must learn to listen even when I am the object of someone's anger. I must listen without editorializing and ask questions in order to find common space.

When I was a second-year teacher, I had Darren Roberts in my class—that bright, energetic, can't-sit-still, can't-stop-hitting, little first-grade boy that you love but who can quickly wreak havoc. I literally had to hold his hand all day in order to try to prevent other children from being hurt.

One day, Darren's dad came into my classroom. He had clearly been drinking and was shouting at me that he was going to have my job. He was upset because I had "allowed" another child to hit

Darren "back." He was raving and furious. Upset and fearful, I sent a child to get the principal. The principal came in and ushered Mr. Roberts out of the room.

About an hour later, the principal asked me into his office. Mr. Roberts was there and had calmed down. The principal asked me to sit while he asked Mr. Roberts what he wanted for Darren's future. Touchingly, Mr. Roberts spoke about the poverty he had grown up in, about how he wanted something more for Darren. He talked about how he had sacrificed to get the very best for his son, how he would do anything to make sure Darren was successful in school, how he wanted Darren to be the first in the family to go to college.

The principal asked me what I wanted for Darren. Mostly, I said the same kinds of things. Then we were able to have a conversation and create an alliance for Darren's future. When the principal asked the right questions and helped me learn to listen with humility, we were able to find the necessary common space to create a new reality.

Look and Listen for Who Is Missing

After years of participating in classes, meetings, and seminars, I have found that it is not sufficient to see who is there and listen to what is said. It is critical to look for who and what are not represented. Is there a group that is left out, either through not having been invited or through choosing not to come? When a marginalized group is not present, an important perspective is missing, and efforts should be made to get that perspective added.

Even when the group present is representative, who is not speaking? What can be done to find out why? Getting that perspective added frequently means having a private conversation with the silent person or group and asking what can be done to get their opinions on the table. Frequently, they have been alienated, and often those doing the alienating are not even aware that they have created an environment in which the marginalized black or poor or immigrant or gay or female people feel unsafe to speak.

Another invisible aspect that should demand our attention is culture. It's often easy to see that a different culture exists, but it is not easy to see one's own. One's own culture is to humans as water is to a fish—we are completely unaware of our culture until we are taken out of it. Those Americans who are part of the dominant culture are seldom outside their own culture and are therefore seldom aware of their culture at all.

Those who bring different experiences to schools are viewed as deficient when assessed through mainstream norms. We are told that we must find out what kids know and don't know so that we can remediate them. The problem, as the great Asa Hilliard once wrote, is that there are two types of questions we could employ. The Type I question asks: "Do you know what I know?" The Type II question asks: "What do you know?"[2]

The first question, "Do you know what I know?" is the culturally charged question that is usually asked in our schools and colleges, the question that makes invisible the culture, the home, the knowledge of the young person in front of us. The very process of trying to find out if a child knows what the school values limits us greatly in seeing our students' abilities.

The second question, "What do you know?" is the question we have to learn to ask. This is the question that will allow us to begin to see all that is invisible in the child before us. This is the question that will allow us to begin, with courage, humility, and cultural sensitivity the right educational journey. This is the question that will help us learn to "help the sheep."

These are the lessons that inform my life's goals and that I have continued to learn over the course of my career. But I have also learned another lesson. We cannot accomplish our personal goals without also devoting attention to how to attain these goals *within* the institutions that so govern our ability to achieve them. This is the question I continue to ask myself. What can I say about the purpose of my life *within* the university? What does being a professor of education at an institution of higher learning mean for me as an African American woman, daughter of a man who received a GED diploma in his fortieth year—a year before my birth—and who died of kidney failure at the age of forty-seven because the "colored ward" was not provided the use of the new dialysis machine in pre-integration Louisiana.

What does it mean for me as a college student of the 1970s, whose political and ethical perspectives were forged against the backdrop of the larger struggle for black liberation and the personal struggle to reconcile the American dream with an American reality as tragic as my father's story. If we aren't here to help the sheep, then what's the point?

When I look at what I spend my days doing, I have to wonder: Am I here to publish in refereed journals? Am I here to read tenure files? To go to meetings? To figure out how to input grades into the new computer program?

Of course I do all those things, but what deeper purpose am I serving? I've come to understand that for me, there must be at least two reasons for dedicating my life to the work I do in the institutions where I do it. The first is that we in education, at universities or in K–12 schools, are charged with preparing the minds and hearts of these who will inherit the earth. I view this as a sacred trust. I believe that, through our students, we shape the world of the future. I further believe that through our teaching we must not only provide technical knowledge, but we must also assure that we fill our students' hearts and minds with the potential for envisioning a future better than we ourselves can even imagine.

Benjamin E. Mays, president of the prestigious, historically black Morehouse College for over twenty-seven years, proclaimed that the purpose of a college education is not only "to train the mind to think, but the heart to feel . . . the injustice of mankind; and to strengthen the will to act in the interest of the common good."[3]

The second purpose of education, I believe, is to build bridges across the great divides, the so-called achievement gap, the technology gap, class divisions, the racial divide. If we do not find a way to bridge the divide between the haves and have-nots, between white and black, between native and immigrant, then we are ensuring our ultimate demise. We are all part of the whole, and no part can be affected without affecting the whole.

Dr. Rudy Crew, former superintendent of the Miami school system, once said that if we are not able to give all of our citizens a future, then the disenfranchised will either implode and destroy themselves or explode in our own front yards and most assuredly destroy us. Education, the potentially great public common ground, can foster the kinds of conversations across cultures, across ethnicities, across classes that can lead to the American ideal we have yet to see realized. Education can un-silence dialogues that are critical for our mutual salvation.

Perhaps uniquely among our public institutions, universities have the potential to help bridge some of these gaps. In his 1869 inaugural address at Harvard, Charles William Eliot asked: "And what will the University do for the community? First, it will make a rich return of learning, poetry, and piety. Secondly, it will foster the sense of public duty—that great virtue which makes republics possible."[4]

I have been pleased to work at universities that define themselves as urban institutions, and at some that even take that role seriously. But there are tensions at many colleges and universities around the country between the desire of faculty and administrators for a larger purpose committed to the needs of the urban community and the actual day-to-day functioning of the educational institution.

Although great individual attention is paid to the important academic work that scholars hope to accomplish, American higher education has not yet found a way to integrate seamlessly the larger purposes of serving the community with individual faculty members' research and scholarship. We haven't, for example, found a consistent, university-wide reward mechanism for building a connection to community and serving those who are technically outside the academy but in whose broader interests universities and all public institutions are actually meant to function.

At Florida International University, as at many universities that serve primarily local populations, the failure rate for freshman algebra is very high: 70 percent. This is not surprising, since many of FIU's students are members of some of the most vulnerable communities in Miami. As the size of freshman classes increases at FIU and other urban universities in response to the economy, we risk raising that failure rate even higher. But what if some of the professors and the grad students who typically teach the labs for larger classes were to learn some of the strategies for teaching algebra that have been so successful in teaching so-called at-risk high school students?

What if some of those freshmen who were challenged by algebra were paid to become college math-literacy workers, as in the Young People's Project of Bob Moses's Algebra Project? Wouldn't they have a much better chance of reviewing the algebraic concepts if they were put in the role of teaching the strategies to high school students? What connections could be made between students, faculty, and the community with such a project?

Ernest Boyer, the late president of the Carnegie Foundation for the Advancement of Teaching, proposed that

> the New American College would organize cross-disciplinary institutes around pressing social issues. Undergraduates at the college would participate in field projects, relating ideas to real life.

Classrooms and laboratories would be extended to include health clinics, youth centers, schools, and government offices. Faculty members would build partnerships with practitioners who would, in turn, come to campus as lecturers and student advisers.[5]

Can you imagine what such institutes might be like? Can you imagine the power of using the community itself as a classroom? As a laboratory? The entire faculty could participate with colleagues across disciplines to focus, with students, on issues facing the microcosm of the world we live in. What would our students learn? That they were connected to the world, that they were important in solving the world's problems. And faculty members would feel a greater sense of humanity and purpose as we pursue our academic goals.

Could the reward system of the university be swayed to value collaboration over individual attainment? Articles that shared information about problems solved with other cities and other communities would be recognized over solely theoretical treatises, for example. In the same vein, I've wondered why we don't have stronger connections among the colleges that address human services. After all, those in the Departments of Education, Social Work, Juvenile Justice, Law, Nursing, and so forth, are often working with the same clients. What could happen if we had an interdisciplinary course in which students from each discipline were exposed to professors from the range of disciplines in a yearlong, community centered, problem-solving course that would gather knowledge of how the client's needs might be addressed from each discipline's perspective? Just think of the models such endeavors could provide for how university students, as future practitioners, might collaborate to solve problems once they are in the workforce.

Elon University in North Carolina initiated what they called Project Pericles in 2002, when Elon became one of ten universities to accept a challenge from the Eugene Lang Foundation to provide a learning experience that would "instill in students an abiding sense of social responsibility and civic concern."[6] In the Periclean Scholars Program, students take part in a series of courses (one per school year), culminating in a class project of global or local social change. Each cohort defines its own project. The class of 2006 chose awareness of the spread of HIV/AIDS in Namibia, Africa, as their project. The class of 2007 chose malnutrition in Honduras. From 2007 to 2010 the students worked in Ghana to improve access to health care and to promote sustainability development. The class of 2011 chose to develop environmental education programs in Sri Lanka, and the class of 2012 will devote its energies to India.

Elon also sponsors service sabbaticals, which allow Elon employees to take part in Project Pericles and to contribute to the community in a significant way. Full-time faculty or staff can apply to be relieved of their university duties for up to one month in order to work for a community organization. Course enhancement grants of a thousand dollars each were awarded to about forty professors to incorporate civic engagement into their classes.

When she was vice president of community involvement at Wheelock College in Boston, Theresa Perry worked with the mayor's office and other institutions in that city to implement a series of faculty-sponsored, interdisciplinary talks and panels about real community problems. Readings were provided for community members and the sessions were advertised in public service announcements. By the third event, there was standing room only in the audience, and community members requested that the series go beyond the few initially planned presentations.

As we seek to institutionalize our commitments to a purposeful university, I believe we must establish an overall plan to engage ourselves with each other, with our students, and with our community. I believe we will come to an even greater understanding that our work can be meaningful only if we figure out how to "help the sheep." As J.C. High Eagle, a Native American leader, has said, if we live life right, we truly understand that we are but spokes on the great wheel of life and that which endangers one spoke endangers the entire wheel. Our work is to strengthen the wheel by strengthening each individual spoke. We are all a part of the wheel. And we are all a part of the flock.

APPENDIX
RECOMMENDED BOOKS TO PROMOTE LITERACY
FOR AFRICAN AMERICAN YOUNG MEN

Compiled by Dr. Alfred W. Tatum

Middle School Level

James Collier and Christopher Collier. *With Every Drop of Blood: A Novel of the Civil War.* New York: Laurel Leaf, 1992.

A fourteen-year-old white boy from Virginia, attempting to bring food to besieged Richmond, is captured by black Union soldiers, one of whom is a former slave his own age. The boys ultimately become friends.

Walter Mosley. *47.* New York: Little, Brown, 2005.

The narrator remembers himself as a young slave named 47 living in Georgia in 1832. A mystical runaway slave called Tall John inspires him to fulfill his destiny and lead his people to freedom.

Walter Dean Myers. *The Beast.* New York: Scholastic, 2003.

A young man leaves his neighborhood in Harlem to attend a college prep school and confronts his anxieties about his future when he returns for winter break to discover that his girlfriend has become addicted to drugs.

———. *Handbook for Boys: A Novel.* New York: HarperTrophy, 2002.

> A sixteen-year-old is given the option of participating in barber Duke Wilson's "community mentoring program" instead of serving time in a youth rehabilitation center. The teen's gradual change in perspective shows the value of adult mentoring.

Gary Paulsen. *Nightjohn.* New York: Laurel Leaf, 1993.

> Nightjohn, a new slave on the Waller plantation, sacrifices his chance for freedom and risks punishment to empower other slaves by helping them learn to read and write.

High School Level

Anthony C. Davis and Jeffrey W. Jackson. *Yo, Little Brother: Basic Rules of Survival for Young African American Males.* Chicago: African American Images, 1998.

> In direct, down-to-earth language, this book offers advice for African American youth from their older counterparts.

Farrah Gray. *Reallionaire: Nine Steps to Becoming Rich from the Inside Out.* Deerfield Beach, FL: HCI, 2005.

> A self-made millionaire and philanthropist at age twenty, the author tells his personal story of growing up on the South Side of Chicago and rising to success.

George Jenkins, Sampson Davis, and Rameck Hunt. *The Pact: Three Young Men Make a Promise and Fulfill a Dream.* New York: Riverhead Books, 2002.

> This true story tells how the three authors grew up in poverty in Newark, New Jersey, became friends at a magnet high school, and made a pact to attend college and become dentists.

Alex Kotlowitz. *There Are No Children Here: The Story of Two Boys Growing Up in the Other America.* New York: Anchor Books, 1991.

A *Wall Street Journal* reporter tells the true story of two brothers, aged eleven and nine, who live in a violence-ridden Chicago housing project.

Walter Mosley. *Workin' on the Chain Gang: Shaking Off the Dead Hand of History.* New York: Ballantine Books, 2000.

This essay about Americans' enslavement to the economy describes a nation ruled by a small power elite and shows what liberation from consumer capitalism might look like.

Ron Suskind. *A Hope in the Unseen: An American Odyssey from the Inner City to the Ivy League.* New York: Random House, 1999.

A *Wall Street Journal* reporter follows an African American through his last two years of high school and his freshman year at Brown University.

Richard Wright. *Rite of Passage.* New York: HarperTrophy, 1994.

Set in Harlem in the late 1940s, this book tells the story of a bright fifteen-year-old boy who suddenly learns that he is a foster child and is being transferred to a new foster home. He runs away and struggles to survive in a harsh world.

Source: "Engaging African American Males in Reading," by Alfred W. Tatum, 2006, *Educational Leadership* 63(5), pp. 44–49. © 2006 by ASCD. Reprinted with permission.

NOTES

Introduction

1. Barbara Ferguson and Karran Harper Royal, "The Deception of the 'Lottery' at Lycée Français and Audubon Schools: The Misuse of Charter Schools—Part II," Research on Reforms, Inc., October 2011. www.researchonreforms.org.

1. There Is No Achievement Gap at Birth

1. Marcelle Geber and R.F.A. Dean, "Gesell Tests on African Children," *Pediatrics* 20 (1957): 1061–64.
2. William K. Frankenburg and Josiah B. Dodds, "The Denver Developmental Screening Test," *Journal of Pediatrics* 71 (1967): 181–91; W.K. Frankenburg, Nathan P. Dick, and James Carland, "Development of Preschool-Aged Children of Different Social and Ethnic Groups: Implications for Developmental Screening," *Journal of Pediatrics* 87

(1975): 125–32; Interview with William Frankenburg and Joe Dodds, December 1988.

3. Kathryn Greaves et al., "Ethnic Differences in Anthropometric Characteristics of Young Children and Their Parents," *Human Biology* 61 (1989): 459–77.

4. Amos Wilson, *The Developmental Psychology of the Black Child* (New York: African Research, 1987).

5. R.K. Payne, *A Framework for Understanding Poverty* (Highlands, TX: aha! Process, 2005).

6. Jawanza Kunjufu, *An African Centered Response to Ruby Payne's Poverty Theory* (Chicago: African American Images, 2006).

7. William Ryan, "Blaming the Victim," in *Race, Class and Gender in the United States*, Paula S. Rothenberg (New York: Macmillan, 2006), 690.

8. William L. Sanders and June C. Rivers, *Cumulative and Residual Effects of Teachers on Future Student Academic Achievement* (Knoxville: University of Tennessee Value-Added Research and Assessment Center, November 1996).

9. Beverly Daniel Tatum, *"Why Are All the Black Kids Sitting Together in the Cafeteria?"* (New York: Basic Books, 1997).

10. Robert B. Moore, *Racism in the English Language* (New York: Racism and Sexism Resource Center for Educators, 1976), 3.

11. Van Jones, "Black People 'Loot' Food . . . White People 'Find' Food, *Huffington Post*, September 1, 2005. Although the Associate Press retracted the "looting" photo and apologized, and the respective photographers defended their choice of wording, the initial publication depicts unedited attitudes.

12. Pedro A. Noguera, *The Trouble with Black Boys* (San Francisco: Jossey-Bass, 2008), 17.

13. Ibid.

14. C. Kirabo Jackson, "Students Demographics, Teacher Sorting, and Teacher Quality: Evidence from the End of School Desegregation," *Journal of Labor Economics* 27, no. 2 (2009): 213–56.

15. *See* Claude Steele, "Stereotype Threat and African American Student Achievement," in *Young, Gifted and Black: Promoting High*

Achievement Among African American Students, ed. Theresa Perry, Claude Steele, and Asa Hilliard III (Boston: Beacon, 2003).

16. *See* C.M. Steele, S.J. Spencer, and J. Aronson, "Contending with Group Image: The Psychology of Stereotype and Social Identity Threat," in *Advances in Experimental Social Psychology,* vol. 34, ed. Mark Zanna (San Diego: Academic Press, 2002).

2. Infinite Capacity

1. Asa Hilliard III, *SBA: The Reawakening of the African Mind* (Gainesville, FL: Makare, 1998).

2. *See* Pierre Erny and Alexander Mboukou, *Childhood and Cosmos* (New York: New Perspectives, 1973).

3. Hilliard, *SBA.*

4. "Overview of the Freedom Schools" in *Freedom School Curriculum* (Mississippi, 1964). Available at http://www.educationanddemocracy.org/FSCfiles/B_09_OverviewOfFSchools.htm.

5. *See* Betty Hart and Todd R. Risley, *Meaningful Differences in the Everyday Experiences of American Children* (Baltimore: Brookes, 1995).

6. Asa G. Hilliard III, "No Mystery: Closing the Achievement Gap Between Africans and Excellence," in *Young, Gifted and Black: Promoting High Achievement Among African American Students,* ed. Theresa Perry, Claude Steele, and Asa Hilliard III (Boston: Beacon, 2003), 131ff.

7. Thomas Toch, "The Education Bazaar," *U.S. News & World Report,* April 27, 1998, 2. http://www.usnews.com/usnews/culture/articles/980427/archive_003791_2.htm.

8. Hilliard, *SBA.*

9. Herbert Kohl, *Stupidity and Tears* (New York: New Press, 2005), 108.

10. Lisa Delpit and Paula White-Bradley, "Educating or Imprisoning the Spirit: Lessons from Ancient Egypt," *Theory Into Practice* 42, no. 4 (2003): 283–88.

11. Kohl, *Stupidity and Tears,* 34–35.

12. *See* Jay R. Campbell et al., *NAEP 1999 Trends in Academic Progress: Three Decades of Student Performance* (Washington, DC: National Center for Education Statistics, 2000), available also at: http://nces.ed.gov/nationsreportcard/pdf/main1999/2000469.pdf; J.S. Chall, V. Jacobs, and L. Baldwin, *Reading Crisis: Why Poor Children Fall Behind* (Cambridge, MA: Harvard Univ. Press, 1990).

13. *See*, for example, I.L. Beck et al., *Bringing Words to Life: Robust Vocabulary Instruction* (New York: Guilford, 2002); S.A. Stahl et al., "Learning Meaning Vocabulary Through Listening: A Sixth-Grade Replication," in *Learner Factors/Teacher Factors: Issues in Literacy Research and Instruction, Fortieth Yearbook of the National Reading Conference,* ed. J. Zutell and S. McCormick (Chicago: National Reading Conference, 1991), 185–92; E.D. Hirsch Jr., "Reading Comprehension Requires Knowledge—of Words and of the World," *American Educator* 27 (Spring 2003); R.J. Sternberg, "Most Vocabulary Is Learned from Context," in *The Nature of Vocabulary Acquisition* ed. M.G. McKeown and M.E. Curtis (Hillsdale, NJ: Erlbaum, 1987); to name but a few.

14. Kohl, *Stupidity and Tears*, 22–23.

15. Theresa Perry, "Up from the Parched Earth: Toward a Philosophy of African-American Achievment," in *Young, Gifted and Black: Promoting High Achievement Among African American Students*, ed. Theresa Perry, Claude Steele, and Asa Hilliard III (Boston: Beacon, 2003).

16. James D. Anderson, *The Education of Blacks in the South, 1860–1935* (Chapel Hill: Univ. of North Carolina Press, 1988).

17. Perry, "Up from the Parched Earth," 11.

18. Ibid., 88.

19. Maya Angelou, *I Know Why the Caged Bird Sings* (New York: Random House, 1969), 152.

20. Ibid., 153.

21. Quoted in Angelou, *I Know Why*, 153.

22. Perry, "Up from the Parched Earth," 49.

23. Angelou, *I Know Why*, 153.

24. Perry, "Up from the Parched Earth."

25. Jacqueline Jordan Irvine, *In Search of Wholeness: African Ameri-*

can Teachers and Their Culturally Specific Classroom Practices (New York: Palgrave, 2003).

26. Ibid.

27. Hilliard, "No Mystery," 152–53.

28. For a fuller description of Secret's teaching, see Theresa Perry and Lisa Delpit, *The Real Ebonics Debate* (Boston: Beacon, 1998), 79–87.

3. Stuff You Never Would Say

1. Theresa Perry, Claude Steele, and Asa Hilliard III, eds., *Young, Gifted and Black: Promoting High Achievement Among African American Students* (Boston: Beacon, 2003.)

2. Tyrone Howard, "Powerful Pedagogy for African American Students: Conceptions of Culturally Relevant Pedagogy," *Urban Education* 36, no. 2 (2001): 195.

3. Hilliard, *SBA*.

4. Joanne Yatvin, Constance Weaver, Elaine Guran, "The Reading First Initiative: Cautions and Recommendations" (undated pamphlet).

5. Michael Grunwald, "Billions for an Inside Game on Reading," *Washington Post,* October 1, 2006. http://www.washingtonpost.com/wp-dyn/content/article/2006/09/29/AR2006092901333.html.

6. Don Holdaway, *Foundations of Literacy* (Portsmouth, NH: Heinemann, 1979), 74

7. W.E. Nagy and P.A. Herman, "Breadth and Depth of Vocabulary Knowledge: Implications for Acquisition and Instruction," in *The Nature of Vocabulary Acquisition*, ed. M.G. McKeown and M.E. Curtis (Hillsdale, NJ: Erlbaum, 1987), 19–35.

8. Kate Kinsella *Preparing for Effective Vocabulary Instruction* (Santa Rosa, CA: Sonoma County Office of Education, 2005).

9. Nagy and Herman, "Breadth and Depth of Vocabulary Knowledge," 19–35.

10. To cite just a few: I. Beck, M. McKeown, and L. Kucan, "Taking Delight in Words," *American Educator* 27 (2003): 36–46. E.D. Hirsch Jr., "Reading Comprehension Requires Knowledge—of Words and the

World," *American Educator* 27 (2003): 10–13, 16–22, 28–29. S.A. Stahl, "Beyond the Instrumentalist Hypothesis: Some Relationships Between Word Meanings and Comprehension," in ed. P. Schwanenflugel, *The Psychology of Word Meanings* (Hillsdale, NJ: Erlbaum, 1991), 157–178. R.J. Sternberg, "Most Vocabulary Is Learned from Context," M.G. McKeown and M.E. Curts, eds., *The Nature of Vocabulary Acquisition* (Hillsdale, NJ: Erlbaum, 1987), 89–106.

4. Warm Demanders

1. Gloria Ladson-Billings, "'Yes, but How Do We Do It?' Practicing Culturally Relevant Pedagogy," in *City Kids, City Schools*, ed. William Ayres, Gloria Ladson-Billings, Gregory Michie, and Peter Noguera (New York: New Press, 2008), 165.

2. Peter Mortimore and Pamela Sammons, "New Evidence of Effective Elementary Schools," *Educational Leadership* 45, no. 1 (September 1987): 4–8.

3. Robert J. Marzano, *What Works in Schools: Translating Research into Action* (Alexandria, VA: Association for Supervision and Curriculum Development, 2003).

4. Mike Schmoker, *Results Now* (Alexandria, VA: Association for Supervision and Curriculum Development, 2006), quoting K. Haycock and S. Huang, "Are Today's High School Graduates Ready?" *Thinking K–16* 5 (Winter 2001): 3–17.

5. Jacqueline Jordan Irvine and James Fraser, "Warm Demanders," *Education Week* 17 (May 13, 1998): 42, 56.

6. Franita Ware, "Warm Demander Pedagogy: Culturally Responsive Teaching That Supports a Culture of Achievement for African American Students," *Urban Education* 41 (July 2006): 436–37.

7. Ibid., 437.

8. Dennis Wholey, *The Miracle of Change* (New York: Simon and Schuster, 1987) 223.

9. Lilly Walters, *Secrets of Superstar Speakers* (New York: McGraw-Hill, 2000).

10. Lisa Delpit, *Other People's Children* (New York: The New Press, 2006), 37.

11. Howard, "Powerful Pedagogy," 139.

12. Ibid., 138.

13. Ibid., 138–39.

14. Valerie Lee et al., *Social Support, Academic Press, and Student Achievement: A View from the Middle Grades in Chicago* (Chicago: Consortium on Chicago School Research, October 1999). http://ccsr .uchicago.edu/publications/p0e01.pdf.

15. Geneva Gay, *Culturally Responsive Teaching: Theory, Research, and Practice* (New York: Teachers College Press, 2000), 109.

16. Michele Foster, *Black Teachers on Teaching* (New York: The New Press, 1997), 49.

17. Ware, "Warm Demander Pedagogy," 438.

18. Jennifer E. Obidah and Karen Manheim Teel, *Because of the Kids: Facing Racial Differences in Schools* (New York: Teachers College Press, 2001).

19. Lisa Delpit, *Other People's Children*, 158.

5. Skin-Deep Learning

1. Pano Rodis, Andrew Garrod, and Mary Lynn Boscardin, eds., *Learning Disabilities and Life Stories* (Boston: Allyn and Bacon, 2000).

2. Lynn Pelkey, in *Learning Disabilities and Life Stories* by Rodis, Garrod, and Boscardin, 18.

3. Gretchen O'Connor, Lynn Pelkey, and Velvet Cunningham, in *Learning Disabilities and Life Stories* by Rodis, Garrod, and Boscardin, 71, 18, 84.

4. A.J. Artiles and S.C. Trent, "Overrepresentation of Minority Students in Special Education: A Continuing Debate," *Journal of Special Education* 27 (1994): 410–37; K.A. Heller, W.H. Holtzman, and S. Messick, eds., *Placing Children in Special Education: A Strategy for Equity* (Washington, DC: National Academies Press, 1982).

5. B. Harry and J.K. Klingner, *Why Are So Many Minority Students*

in Special Education? Understanding Race and Disability in Schools (New York: Teachers College Press, 2006).

6. C.M. Steele and J. Aronson, "Stereotype Threat and the Intellectual Performance of African Americans," *Journal of Personality and Social Psychology* 69, no. 5 (1995): 797–811.

7. Ibid.

8. Rodis, Garrod, and Boscardin, 20.

9. Rodis, Garrod, and Buscardin, 21.

10. Herbert Kohl and Tom Oppenheim, *The Muses Go to School* (New York: The New Press, 2012), 38.

6. "I Don't Like It When They Don't Say My Name Right"

1. Greg Toppo, "Reflections: 50 Years After *Brown vs. Board of Education*," *USA Today*, May 14, 2004; updated May 17, 2004. http://www .usatoday.com/news/nation/2004-05-14-50-years-after-brown_x.htm.

2. Ibid.

3. Ibid.

4. J.K. Haynes, "Veteran Educator Bemoans Loss of Negro Teachers and Principals," *Baton Rouge Sunday Advocate*, October 6, 1968.

5. "La. Teacher Situation Probe Slated by Group," *State Times* (Baton Rouge), February 17, 1970.

6. Johnny Butler, "Black Educators in Louisiana—a Question of Survival," *Journal of Negro Education* 43 (Winter 1974): 9–24.

7. *Adams v. Rankin County Board of Education*, 485 F.2d 324 (5th Cir., 1973).

8. Quoted in Butler, "Black Educators in Louisiana," 18.

9. Quoted in Butler, "Black Educators in Louisiana," 19.

10. Amanda Ripley, "Rhee Tackles Classroom Challenge," *Time*, December 8, 2008. http://www.time.com/time/magazine/article/0 ,9171,1862444-1,00.html.

11. Valerie Strauss, "Ravitch: The Problem with Teach for America," *Washington Post Answer Sheet* blog, February 15, 2011. http://voices

.washingtonpost.com/answer-sheet/diane-ravitch/ravitch-the-problem
-with-teach.html.

12. Greg Toppo, "Teach for America: Elite Corps or Costing Older
Teachers Jobs?" *USA Today*, July 29, 2009, quoted in Barbara Miner,
"Looking Past the Spin: Teach for America," *Rethinking Schools* 24,
no. 3 (Spring 2010).

13. Bill Turque and Emma Brown, "D.C. Schools Lay Off More
than 220 Teachers, Lose 300 Guards," *Washington Post*, October 3,
2009. http://www.washingtonpost.com/wp-dyn/content/article/2009
/10/02/AR2009100202289.html.

14. Rachel Monahan, "Amid Threat of Layoffs, City Is Recruiting
500 New Teachers for Next Fall," *New York Daily News*, May 19, 2011.
http://www.nydailynews.com/2011-05-19/local/29576241_1_new
-teachers-laid-off-teachers-shortage-areas; accessed 7/31/2011.

15. "Teach for America and Teacher Layoffs in Kansas City," *Education
State*, April 27, 2011. http://www.educationstate.org/2011/04/27/
teach-america-teacher-layoffs-kansas-city.

16. James Haug, "Teachers Wary of Recruitment Group," *Las Vegas
Review-Journal*, July 7, 2011. http://www.lvrj.com/news/teachers-wary-
of-recruitment.

17. Michael Reed. "After the Layoffs, HISD Now Needs Teachers,"
The Examiner.com, May 10, 2011. http://www.yourhoustonnews.com/
west_university/news/article_bffb1ed7-3b66-5949-80.

18. Quoted in Barbara Miner, "Looking Past the Spin: Teach for
America," *Rethinking Schools* 24, no. 3 (Spring 2010). http://www
.rethinkingschools.org/archive/24_03/24_03_TFA.shtml.

19. Office of the Governor of Alabama, "Teach for America Expand-
ing to Alabama, Bringing 90 Dedicated Teachers to the Black Belt in
the Next Three Years," news release, February 18, 2010.

20. Personal communication with Lance Hill.

21. Darran Simon, "Millions Headed to N.O. Schools," *New Orleans
Times-Picayune*, December 12, 2007. http://www.nola.com/news/index
.ssf/2007/12/millions_headed_for_no_schools.html.

22. Julian Vaszquez Heilig and Su Jin Jez, "Teach for America: A

Review of the Evidence," National Education Policy Center, June 2010. http://epicpolicy.org/publication/teach-for-america.

23. E.A. Hanushek, J.F. Kain, D.M. O'Brien, and S.G. Rivkin, "The Market for Teacher Quality," National Bureau of Economic Research, Working Paper No. 11154, February 2005. http://ssrn.com /abstract=669453.

7. Picking Up the Broom

1. Martin Haberman, "The Pedagogy of Poverty Versus Good Teaching," *Phi Delta Kappan* 74, no. 4 (December 1991): 290–94.

2. Mike Schmoker, "The 'Crayola Curriculum,'" *Education Week*, October 24, 2001. http://mikeschmoker.com/crayola-curriculum.html.

3. Schmoker, "The 'Crayola Curriculum.'"

4. Schmoker, "The 'Crayola Curriculum.'"

5. Amy Wilkins and the Education Trust Staff, *Yes, We Can: Telling Truths and Dispelling Myths About Race and Education in America* (Washington, DC: Education Trust, September 2006), 8–9. http:// www.edtrust.org/sites/edtrust.org/files/publications/files/YesWeCan .pdf.

6. Bill Bigelow and Linda Christensen, "Write to Think: Teaching about Social Conflict Through Imaginative Writing," in *The Writing Notebook*, ed. S. Franklin and J. Madian (Eugene, OR: The Writing Notebook, 1987), 11–14.

7. Ibid., 13.

8. Ibid., 14.

9. Carter G. Woodson, *The Mis-education of the Negro* (1933; Radford, VA: Wilder, 2008), 7–8.

10. Lucy Calkins, Kate Montgomery, and Donna Santman, with Beverly Falk, *A Teacher's Guide to Standardized Reading Tests: Knowledge Is Power* (Portsmith, NH: Heinemann, 1998), 51–53.

11. Richard L. Allington, *What Really Matters for Struggling Readers: Designing Research-Based Programs* (New York: Longman, 2001).

12. Quoted in Schmoker, *Results Now*, 91.

13. Cf. Schmoker, *Results Now*; Allington, *What Really Matters*;

Calkins, Montgomery, and Santman, *A Teacher's Guide to Standardized Reading Tests.*

14. Cited in Schmoker, *Results Now*, 97.

15. Asa Hilliard III, "Do We Have the Will to Educate All Children?" *Educational Leadership* 49, no. 1 (1991): 31.

16. Ibid., p. 32

17. Haberman, "Pedagogy of Poverty," 293–94.

8. How Would a Fool Do It?

1. Michael Cole, *Cultural Psychology: A Once and Future Discipline* (Cambridge, MA: Belknap Press of Harvard Univ. Press, 1996), quoted in Malcolm Gladwell, "None of the Above," Books, *New Yorker*, December 17, 2007. http://www.gladwell.com/2007/2007_12_17_c_iq.html.

2. Vivian Gussin Paley, *White Teacher*, 2nd ed. (Cambridge, MA: Harvard Univ. Press, 2000), 72.

3. Shirley Brice Heath, *Ways with Words: Language, Life and Work in Communities and Classrooms* (New York: Cambridge University Press, 1983), 108.

4. Wayne Dyer, *The Power of Intention* (Carlsbad, CA: Hay House, 2004).

5. Personal communication.

6. Personal communication with Asa Hilliard III.

7. Schmoker, *Results Now*, 10.

8. Ibid., 25.

9. Ibid.

10. James W. Stigler and James Hiebert, *The Teaching Gap: Best Ideas from the World's Teachers for Improving Education in the Classroom*, Rep. ed (New York: Free Press, 2009), xviii–xix.

11. Schmoker, *Results Now*, 122.

9. Shooting Hoops

1. David Shenk, *The Genius in All of Us: New Insights into Genetics, Talent and IQ* (New York: Anchor Books, 2011), 84.

2. Quoted in Shenk, *The Genius in All of Us*, 84.

3. Edmund Morris, *Beethoven, the Universal Composer* (New York: HarperCollins, 2005), 16.

4. Shinichi Suzuki, *Nurtured by Love: The Classic Approach to Talent Education* (Winnetka, IL: Suzuki Method International; distributed by Warner Brothers, 1986; Kindle ed.), 20.

5. Quoted in Shenk, *The Genius in All of Us*, 34–35.

6. Adair F. White-Johnson, "'Peas 'n' Rice' or 'Rice 'n' Peas'—Which One Are We Really Ordering? The Plight of African American Male Students Engaged in Educational Exchange Processes," *Urban Education* 36, no. 3 (May 2001): 343–73.

7. Alfred Tatum, "Engaging African American Males in Reading," *Educational Leadership* 63, no. 5 (February 2006): 45.

8. Quoted in Tatum, "Engaging African American Males in Reading," 45.

9. Tatum, "Engaging African American Males in Reading," 46.

10. Eric Gutstein and Bob Peterson, eds., *Rethinking Mathematics: Teaching Social Justice by the Numbers* (Milwaukee: Rethinking Schools, 2005), 1.

11. Quoted on the Urban Prep Academies website. http://www.urbanprep.org/about/creed.asp.

12. Unpublished printed document provided by school.

13. Claude M. Steele, "Race and the Schooling of Black Americans," *Atlantic Monthly,* April 1992.

10. Invisibility, Disidentification, and Negotiating Blackness on Campus

1. Anderson J. Franklin, "Invisibility Syndrome and Racial Identity Develoment in Psychotherapy and Counseling African American Men," *Counseling Psychologist* 27, no. 6 (1999): 761–93.

2. Lance Hill, "The New Orleans Convention Center Disaster: Incompetence or Racism?" *Commentaries by Lance Hill* (blog archive), August 22, 2006. http://www.southerninstitute.info/commentaries/?m=200608&paged=2.

3. Ibid.

4. Charles Babington, "Some GOP Legislators Hit Jarring Notes in Addressing Katrina," *Washington Post*, September 10, 2005.

5. *See* Gordon J. Beggs, "Novel Expert Evidence in Federal Civil Rights Litigation," *American University Law Review* 45 (October 1995). http://www.wcl.american.edu/journal/lawrev/45/beggstxt.html.

6. Patricia Williams, *Seeing a Color Blind Future: The Paradox of Race* (New York: Farrar, Straus & Giroux, 1998), 38–40.

7. Chester M. Pierce et al., "An Experiment in Racism: TV Commercials," in *Television and Education*, ed., Chester M. Pierce (Beverly Hills, CA: Sage, 1978), 62–88.

8. Derald Wing Sue et al., "Racial Microagression in Everyday Life: Implications for Clinical Practice," *American Psychologist* 62, no. 4 (2007): 27.

9. "College Graduation Rates: Where Black Students Do the Best and Where They Fare Poorly Compared to Their White Peers," *Journal of Blacks in Higher Education*, May 15, 2011. http://www.jbhe.com /features/65_gradrates.html.

10. Claude M. Steele, "Race and the Schooling of Black Americans," *Atlantic*, April 1992. http://www.theatlantic.com/magazine/archive /1992/04/race-and-the-schooling-of-black-americans/6073/.

11. J.R. Ancis, W.E Sedlacek, and J.J Mohr, "Student Perceptions of Campus Cultural Climates by Race," *Journal of Counseling and Development* 78 (Spring 2000): 180–85.

12. A.F. Cabrera and A. Nora, "College Students' Perceptions of Prejudice and Discrimination and Their Feelings of Alienation: A Construct Validation Approach," *Review of Education, Pedagogy, and Cultural Studies* 16 (1994): 387–409.

13. Beverly Daniel Tatum, *"Why Are All the Black Kids Sitting Together in the Cafeteria?": And Other Conversations About Race*, Rev. ed. (New York: Basic Books, 2003), 78.

14. Steele, "Race and the Schooling of Black Americans."

15. Jacqueline Fleming, *Blacks in College: A Comparative Study of Students' Success in Black and in White Institutions* (San Francisco:

Jossey-Bass, 1984), quoted in Steele, "Race and the Schooling of Black Americans."

16. Steele, "Race and the Schooling of Black Americans."

17. Ibid.

18. Loren Pope, *Colleges That Change Lives: 40 Schools That Will Change the Way You Think About Colleges* (New York: Penguin, 2006).

19. Fullilove and Treisman, "Mathematics Achievement Among African American Undergraduates."

20. Hollis Duncan and Dick Thomas, "Collaborative Workshops and Student Academic Performance in Introductory College Mathematics Courses: A Study of a Treisman Model Math Excel Program," in *School Science and Mathematics* 100, no. 7 (November 2000): 365–73.

21. Steele, "Race and the Schooling of Black Americans."

22. Michele Foster, "It's Cookin' Now: An Ethnographic Study of the Teaching Style of a Successful Black Teacher in an Urban Community College" (PhD diss., Harvard University, 1987) 32.

23. Ibid., 38.

11. Will It Help the Sheep?

1. Sol Worth and John Adair, *Through Navajo Eyes: An Exploration in Film Communication and Anthropology* (Albuquerque: University of New Mexico Press, 1997).

2. Asa G. Hilliard III, *Alternatives to IQ Testing: An Approach to the Identification of Gifted "Minority" Children*, Final report (Sacramento: California State Department of Education, June 1976).

3. Benjamin E. Mays, *Born to Rebel: An Autobiography* (Athens, University of Georgia Press, 1971), xxxviii.

4. *Addresses at the Inauguration of Charles William Eliot as President of Harvard College, Tuesday, October 19, 1869* (Cambridge, MA: Sever and Francis), 64.

5. Ernest Boyer, "Creating the New American College," *Chronicle of Higher Education*, March 9, 1994: A48.

6. Elon University, "Project Pericles," http://www.elon.edu/e-web /academics/special_programs/project_pericles/.

OTHER EDUCATION TITLES
AVAILABLE FROM THE NEW PRESS

Be Honest: And Other Advice from Students Across the Country
Edited by Nínive Calegari
From 826 National

826 National co-founder and former CEO Nínive Calegari presents a riveting book full of surprising insights from young people who have a lot to say to their teachers.

Beyond the Bake Sale: The Essential Guide to Family-School
  Partnerships
Anne T. Henderson, Karen L. Mapp, Vivian R. Johnson, and Don Davies

A practical, hands-on primer for helping schools and families work better together to improve children's education.

Black Teachers on Teaching
Michele Foster

An honest and compelling account of the politics and philosophies involved in the education of black children during the last fifty years. Michele Foster talks to those who were the first to teach in desegregated southern schools and to others who taught in large urban districts, such as Boston, Los Angeles, and Philadelphia. All go on record about the losses and gains accompanying desegregation, the inspirations and rewards of teaching, and the challenges and solutions they see in the coming years.

The Case for Make Believe: Saving Play in a Commercialized World
Susan Linn

A clarion call for rescuing creative play from the grips of commercialism.

City Kids, City Schools: More Reports from the Front Row
Edited by William Ayers, Gloria Ladson-Billings, Gregory Michie, and Pedro A. Noguera

A contemporary companion to *City Kids, City Teachers*, this new and timely collection has been compiled by four of the country's most prominent urban educators. Contributors including Sandra Cisneros, Jonathan Kozol, Sapphire, and Patricia J. Williams provide some of the best writing on life in city schools and neighborhoods.

City Kids, City Teachers: Reports from the Front Row
Edited by William Ayers and Patricia Ford

Reissued with a new introduction by William Ayers that reflects on how improving urban education is more essential than ever, this book has become a touchstone for urban educators, exploding the stereotypes of teaching in the city. In more than twenty-five provocative selections, set in context by Ayers and Ford, an all-star cast of educators and writers explores the surprising realities of city classrooms from kindergarten through high school.

Classroom Conversations: A Collection of Classics for Parents and Teachers
Edited by Alexandra Miletta and Maureen Miletta

An outstanding collection of classic readings on teaching and learning from Dewey to Delpit—the age-old ritual of the parent-teacher conference will never be the same again.

Crossing the Tracks: How "Untracking" Can Save America's Schools
Anne Wheelock

A highly praised study of ways in which schools have experimented with heterogeneous groupings in the classroom.

Dismantling Desegregation: The Quiet Reversal of Brown v. Board of Education
Gary Orfield and Susan E. Eaton

Dismantling Desegregation explains the consequences of resegregation and offers a more constructive path toward an equitable future. By citing case studies of ten school districts across the country, Orfield and Eaton uncover the demise of what many feel have been the only legally enforceable routes of access and opportunity for millions of school children in America.

Everyday Antiracism: Getting Real About Race in School
Edited by Mica Pollock

Leading experts offer concrete and realistic strategies for dealing with race in schools in a groundbreaking book offering invaluable and effective advice.

Fires in the Bathroom: Advice for Teachers from High School Students
Kathleen Cushman

Kathleen Cushman's groundbreaking book offers original insights into teaching teenagers in today's hard-pressed urban high schools from the point of view of the students themselves. It speaks to both new and established teachers, giving them firsthand information about who their students are and what they need to succeed.

Fires in the Middle School Bathroom: Advice for Teachers from Middle School Students
Kathleen Cushman and Laura Rogers

This invaluable resource provides a unique window into how middle school students think, feel, and learn, bringing their needs to the forefront of the conversation about education.

Going Public: Schooling for a Diverse Democracy
Judith Renyi

A historically informed overview of the multicultural education debate from a leading advocate.

"I Won't Learn from You": And Other Thoughts on Creative Maladjustment
Herbert Kohl

Herb Kohl's now-classic essay on "not learning," or refusing to learn, along with four other landmark essays.

Kindergarten: A Teacher, Her Students, and a Year of Learning
Julie Diamond

Written for parents and teachers alike, *Kindergarten* offers a rare glimpse into what's really going on behind the apparent chaos of a busy kindergarten classroom, sharing much-needed insights into how our children can have the best possible early school experiences.

Lies My Teacher Told Me: Everything Your American History Textbook Got Wrong
James W. Loewen

Beginning with pre-Columbian history and ranging over characters and events as diverse as Reconstruction, Helen Keller, the first Thanksgiving, and the My Lai massacre, Loewen offers an eye-opening critique of existing textbooks, and a wonderful retelling of American history as it should—and could—be taught to American students.

Lies My Teacher Told Me About Christopher Columbus: What Your History Books Got Wrong
James W. Loewen

The bestselling author of *Lies My Teacher Told Me* offers a graphic corrective to the Columbus story told in so many American classrooms.

The Lost Soul of Higher Education: Corporatization, the Assault on Academic Freedom, and the End of the American University
Ellen Schrecker

A sharp riposte to the conservative critics of the academy by the leading historian of the McCarthy-era witch hunts, *The Lost Soul of Higher Education* reveals a system in peril—and with it the vital role of higher education in our democracy.

Made in America: Immigrant Students in Our Public Schools
Laurie Olsen

Made in America describes Madison High, a prototypical public high school, where more than 20 percent of students were born in another country and more than a third speak limited English or come from homes in which English is not spoken. Through interviews with teachers, administrators, students, and parents, Olsen explores such issues as the complexities of bilingual education and the difficulties of dating for students already promised in marriage at birth.

The Muses Go to School: Inspiring Stories About the Importance of Arts in Education
Edited by Herbert Kohl and Tom Oppenheim

Celebrated artists and educators make a compelling case that the arts belong at the heart of the American education system—an eloquent answer to those who think high standards don't include the arts.

The New Press Education Reader: Leading Educators Speak Out
Edited by Ellen Gordon Reeves

The New Press Education Reader brings together the work of progressive writers and educators—among them Lisa Delpit, Herbert Kohl, William Ayers, and Maxine Greene—to discuss the most pressing and challenging issues now facing us, including schools and social justice, equity issues, tracking and testing, combating racism and homophobia, closing the achievement gap, children in poverty, faculty retention and recruitment, multicultural and bilingual education, rethinking history, and the effects of consumerism on children.

Other People's Children: Cultural Conflict in the Classroom
Lisa Delpit

Winner of an American Educational Studies Association Critics' Choice Award, *Choice Magazine*'s Outstanding Academic Book Award, and voted one of *Teacher Magazine*'s "great books," *Other People's Children* develops ideas about ways teachers can be better "cultural transmitters" in the classroom, where prejudice, stereotypes, and cultural assumptions breed ineffective education.

Out of the Classroom and into the World: Learning from Field Trips, Educating from Experience, and Unlocking the Potential of Our Students and Teachers
Salvatore Vascellaro

An accessible new resource for educators everywhere that eloquently makes the case for letting children and teachers out of the classroom to open their minds to learning.

Rethinking Schools: An Agenda for Change
Edited by David Levine, Robert Lowe, Robert Peterson, and Andrita Tenorio

Rethinking Schools includes sections on rethinking language arts and social studies curricula, testing and tracking, national education policy, antibias and multicultural education, and building school communities. These articles are practical essays by classroom teachers as well as educators such as Henry Louis Gates Jr., Bill Bigelow, Lisa D. Delpit, and Howard Zinn.

She Would Not Be Moved: How We Tell the Story of Rosa Parks and the Montgomery Bus Boycott
Herbert Kohl

The prizewinning educator's brilliant and timely meditation on the misleading ways in which we teach the story of Rosa Parks.

Should We Burn Babar? Essays on Children's Literature and the Power of Stories
Herbert Kohl

Beginning with the title essay on Babar the elephant—"just one of a fine series of inquiries into the power children's books have to shape cultural attitudes," according to *Elliott Bay Booknotes*—the book includes essays on Pinocchio, the history of progressive education, and a call for the writing of more radical children's literature.

The Skin That We Speak: Thoughts on Language and Culture in the Classroom
Edited by Lisa Delpit and Joanne Kilgour Dowdy

The author of *Other People's Children* joins with other experts to examine the relationship between language and power in the classroom.

Stupidity and Tears: Teaching and Learning in Troubled Times
Herbert Kohl

A call to arms against the increasingly hostile climate of public education. Among the topics explored by Kohl are the pressures of standards-based assessments and harrowing sink-or-swim policies, the pain teachers feel when asked to teach against their pedagogical conscience, the development of a capacity to sense how students perceive the world, and the importance of hope and creativity in strengthening the social imagination of students and teachers.

Teachers Have It Easy: The Big Sacrifices and Small Salaries of America's Teachers
Daniel Moulthrop, Nínive Calegari, and Dave Eggers

With a look at the problems of recruitment and retention, the myths of short workdays and endless summer vacations, the realities of the workweek, and shocking examples of how society views America's teachers, *Teachers Have It Easy*—the basis of the documentary *American Teacher*—explores the best ways to improve public education and transform our schools.

Teaching for Social Justice: A Democracy and Education Reader
Edited by William Ayers, Jean Ann Hunt, and Therese Quinn

A popular handbook on teaching social justice for parents and educators, featuring a unique mix of hands-on, historical, and inspirational writings. Topics covered include education through social action, writing and community building, and adult literacy.

Why School? Reclaiming Education for All of Us
Mike Rose

A powerful and timely exploration of this country's education goals, and how they are put into practice, by the award-winning author and educator.

Zero Tolerance: Resisting the Drive for Punishment in Our Schools
Edited by William Ayers, Bernardine Dohrn, and Rick Ayers

Zero Tolerance assembles prominent educators and intellectuals, including the Rev. Jesse L. Jackson Sr., Michelle Fine, and Patricia J. Williams, along with teachers, students, and community activists, to show that the vast majority of students expelled from schools under new disciplinary measures are sent home for nonviolent violations; that the rush to judge and punish disproportionately affects black and Latino children; and that the new disciplinary ethos is eroding constitutional protections of privacy, free speech, and due process.